A Year of Creativity

A YEAR OF CREATIVITY
a seasonal guide to new awareness

Brenda Mallon

MQP

Published by MQ Publications Ltd
12 The Ivories
6–8 Northampton Street
London N1 2HY
Tel: 020 7359 2244
Fax: 020 7359 1616
Email: mail@mqpublications.com

Series Editor: Ljiljana Baird
Designer: Tracy Timson

ISBN: 1-84072-332-7
1 2 3 4 5 6 7 8 9

Printed in France.

Contents

Introduction

A Year of Creativity takes us on a journey of mind, body, and spirit to awaken the creative self. An inspired, interactive workbook, it is filled with practical techniques designed to liberate our creativity and improve the physical, emotional, and spiritual quality of our lives. Creativity is about using our ability to make and create in an original way. It is not about making the perfect painting or writing the best poem, but letting your imagination lead you to original ideas. If you have ever felt inhibited about creating something or felt that you are not creative—that you can't do it—then this book will show you how. It is easy to understand, practical, and based on the truth that we are all creative and that with patience and sensitive support we can all discover the artist within.

Sometimes you will find that you immediately experience a heightened sense of creativity. However, at other times you will undergo a slower, more gentle development, like the uncurling of a seed as it sends out shoots toward the sun. It eventually blossoms but it takes time. However long it takes, the process of creativity is as important as the final product—in many cases, more important. By doing the exercises, reflecting on the activities, and writing up your experiences thoughtfully you will learn more about yourself and what you need in your life. You may open up lots of new creative possibilities to yourself that reveal an inspirational dimension that you never dreamed of before.

Within every individual there is a secret real self, a spiritual core rich in creative potential, that is responsible for our sudden insights, profound emotional responses, and the release of creative energy. Using an easy-to-follow format, *A Year of Creativity* presents twelve creative paths, one for each month, which enable us to discover and enhance different aspects of the creative being within. These include guided exercises to help stimulate our intuitive abilities, extend self-awareness, and explore different routes to creativity. Each path gives us a deeper awareness of self, and of our personal talents, while encouraging us to feel more confident about our creative abilities.

Each creative path contains short sections, including a brief questionnaire. Remember—there are no right or wrong answers. Whatever you do is right because this book is all about discovering the creative side of *you*. Each questionnaire gives you feedback and a chance to reflect on your answers. It also gives you suggestions for follow-up or ideas from others who have answered similar questions. All of these things are designed to build your creative confidence. In answering the questionnaire be as honest and spontaneous as you can. In this way you will gain maximum benefit. The questionnaire is for your development so shut off the censor in your mind that says "That's not right." Remember, whatever you reply is right for you.

After you complete the questionnaire you move on to a series of exercises with live examples to guide you on your way. At the end of the first six sections we take stock, look back at what you created, what you enjoyed, and what you have learned about your creative self.

I have suggested that you keep a Creative Year Journal. This is for you alone, though if you choose to show it to others that is a gift to them. Be completely open and honest as you write in it, and do not feel anxious lest anyone read or make adverse or flippant comments. Entries to this journal will help you on your creative path and in the final section of the book you will reflect on all the activities completed. Ultimately, this will help you to recognize your strengths and abilities. It will also show you how to go further in your search for self-expression.

This seasonal journey toward our creative heart involves all the senses and draws on an eclectic array of sources: high art, nature, everyday objects, inspirational quotes, humor, and our own spontaneous input.

We will explore the growth in spring when fresh energy and early learning takes place. Creative Inspiration reveals how we can develop our intuition, while in Creative Mapping we look at starting points and life's paths. In Creative Myth-making we discover the importance of stories to our fundamental selves.

We will look at how our ideas flower and develop in the summer sunshine. Creative Drawing reveals that we are all artists waiting to blossom, like buds on a tree. Creative Visualization will help us to appreciate the wealth of possibilities that are open to us in our lives.

In fall, we harvest and reap the benefits of our efforts. In Creative Color we celebrate the rich variety of shades that brighten our fall trees, and see how this is mirrored in our lives and the colors that influence our moods and express our personalities. In Creative Abundance we learn how to recognize the gifts of fall every day and to create ways to attract greater physical, spiritual, and emotional wealth.

In the final section, we will look at the importance of winter, a time of completion, when the dormant earth protects the seeds of new growth, when we reflect deeply on our place in the cycle of life, in the cycle of creation of which we are an integral part. We learn that winter is as essential as every other season and that the cycles of our existence each have a valuable part to play in our creative development.

Brenda Mallon

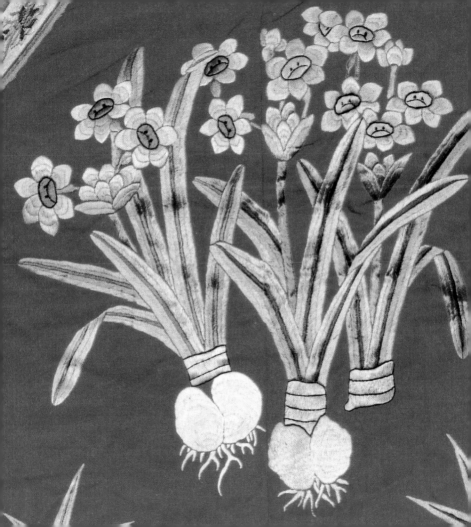

PLANTING

At the beginning of our creative journey our creative mind bursts into life like the earth after its long winter sleep. Our first faltering steps toward goals still hazy and ever-changing are taken during this initial phase. In Creative Inspiration, Creative Mapping, and Creative Myth-making we look for the seeds of inspiration within ourselves, which are yearning to produce shoots and force their way up into the fresh new air.

Month 1

Creative Inspiration

Inspiration means to breathe life into, to invigorate, to arouse. In the repetitive activities and habitual responses that dominate so many waking hours, the spark of creativity can become dulled. This chapter presents exercises to help you look for your originality within—for the source of the first path in every creative journey is the Self—and to find inspiration from your relationship to the outside world.

In Creative Inspiration you will discover how to use the natural world to access the original source of life within you, adding meaning to everyday objects and situations. All too often we overlook this spark of insight, yet as you go into the heart of your feelings and intuition you extract nuggets of brilliance you might previously have ignored. Here we will consider ways to enhance your intuitive sensitivity so you are not misled by the dullness of unpolished diamonds, those intuitive flashes, but can see deeper into their worth.

Inspiration brings transformation. It may be a short or a long process; it takes the time it needs, just as each seed or bulb has its own gestation period. You will need to set aside some time each week to give yourself space to grow and change. When you become more aware of your inspiration you become freer, more spontaneous, and feel the zest of life.

The first path

ONE – UNITY.
SELF.

> *You are a child of the universe, no less than the trees and the stars.*
> *You have a right to be here.* DESIDERATA

The number one symbolizes the spiritual unity that joins all beings. It represents wholeness, but paradoxically one also describes something that is distinct from all others, or unique. As you travel down this first path you will discover more about what makes you special, what makes you one in a billion, and you will find new connections with the wider world.

The power of one is a creative energy that governs all first things. It symbolizes the beginning, the starting point, the initial move. As you take your first steps on your journey toward greater creativity it is important to be aware of your Self—acknowledge your experiences, your thoughts, and your unique voice.

It is helpful to think about the "first" times in your life, and how they made you feel. Were you confident or afraid of making a mistake? Did you need to make lots of preparations or did you just jump in and have a go? When you meditate on your attitudes you learn more about what makes for success and what stifles your creativity. Make a list of your first time experiences in your Creative Year Journal. Record your fears, feelings of joy, and what was so special about each of these first times.

Questionnaire

The aim of these questions is to help you reflect on the conditions that affect you now—what makes you happy and what hinders your progress—and then to put you in touch with your inner resources, for instance, your resilience to carry on when you are faced with difficulties or to recognize that you have the stamina to follow up your own good ideas.

* When was the last time you had a flash of inspiration, an unexpected idea, or a hunch that proved correct or led you to an important recognition? *CAN'T REMEMBER*

* What feelings, physical and emotional, did you have? *EXCITEMENT ENERGY.*

* Who inspires you? *— NO-ONE*

* What is your most creative time of day? *MORNING*

* Can you name a place that has been a source of inspiration for you? *WHENEVER I GO SOMEWHERE I HAVE IDEAS*

* If you are inspired to do something, what is your first response?

* When you are fired up with an idea, do you follow through? *NO !!!* *EXCITEMENT CAN'T STOP ME GOING TO WORK*

my garden. make it more so

15

Feedback

- Inspiration can come at any time. The essential thing is to be open to it and to take those flashes of brilliance seriously when they arrive.

- A flash of inspiration is typically accompanied by feelings of excitement, nervousness, euphoria, and a "wow" response. Note your emotional and physical response to inspiration to help you recognize the signals next time you are inspired.

- Friends, family, and people in the public eye inspire us. Whether it is a person who has survived incredible odds or someone who has produced something remarkable, what they have in common is a sense of determination and a belief in themselves. Cherish those who inspire you and, if it is someone you know, make sure that you let her or him know how much you appreciate his or her inspirational qualities.

- Are you a lark or an owl? If you know that mornings are your best time, then try to use that space to work on anything that needs an inspirational, creative approach. Keep routine tasks for times when you are not quite so switched on.

- Places are often inspirational. Whether you thought of somewhere remote, such as the Gobi Desert or the Himalayas, or somewhere more accessible, such as a local park or beauty spot, what is significant is that your chosen space works for you. Having identified it, ask yourself whether you visit it often enough. Think about what it was that made it special to you—what inspired you. If your visit was a once-in-a-lifetime journey, what place can you find locally that shares some of the same characteristics? The lonely peaks of your nearest mountain range may recapture the spirituality of the Himalayas. All future places you visit are potentially inspirational, so be ready to embrace their opportunities.

- Your first response to a flash of inspiration is crucial. Sometimes, immediately after a great idea strikes, so does doubt. "It will never work," "I'm not much good at this type of thing so I won't say anything," or "What if I'm wrong? I'll look a fool." Such negativity can be replaced by a positive self-talk habit with a bit of perseverance, patience, and discipline. Once you start believing in yourself the cycle of success has begun.

- When you are enthused with a new idea, follow it through. If you create the right environment to continue, establish discipline, and set time aside to complete your project, you are much more likely to succeed—and you'll probably enjoy yourself in the process.

This questionnaire helps you to harness your inspiration and make space for your creativity in practical ways. Most creative activity is ten percent inspiration and ninety percent perspiration! Many successful writers, artists, and business people say that having the idea is the first step but without hard work and dogged perseverance there would be nothing to show for it. When you have an idea, write it down in a notebook and promise yourself fifteen minutes that day when you will try to develop it. Once you have established this habit you will find your creative side eagerly awaiting the opportunity to pour forth yet more inspiration.

Your inner landscape

Landscape: an extensive area of scenery as viewed from a single aspect.

To landscape: to improve the natural features of, for example, a garden or park, by creating new features or contours.

Your inner landscape is the one inside your head. It consists of your moods, thoughts, personality, and hopes. Just like a physical landscape it is formed by history—by eruptions, scarring, and drought—which in emotional terms may be a personal catastrophe such as bereavement, wounds from a failed relationship, or enduring a period of loneliness. Your inner landscape reflects all your experiences and it provides the basis for future development.

Just as through judicious earthworks and planting we can transform a natural landscape, so we can alter our inner landscape by building on our strengths, nurturing our best features, and getting rid of the things that hamper us. Before you can change, however, you have to know what your inner landscape is like. Think about your strengths, skills, personality, and achievements. Make three lists: "What I like about myself;" "What I would like to change;" and "What I can learn to accept."

If you are having trouble with the first list, maybe your critical censor—that internal authority figure that criticizes and complains—needs to be switched off. Shut out thoughts such as "You're no good" and "You'll never succeed." Remind yourself that it is your right to experiment and play, and that creativity is a process, not just a finished picture on a wall. This is your life; you can choose to do things differently.

When you've completed your list, celebrate your wonderful qualities. Recognize the positive changes you have already made in your life; acknowledge the trials you have successfully overcome. Celebrate the fact that the health, looks, and personality that you inherited have sustained you until now and have given you joy. Concentrate on the positive moments in your life and let the negative ones melt like snow in the sun.

Celebrate the wisdom of accepting what you cannot change, because it is one of the hardest things to do. We are all flawed; we would not be human if we did not have some weaknesses. By exchanging "if only" for "it's happened and I can't change it" you begin to let go and free yourself for the future.

Look at the list of things you want to change and think of ways to bring such change about. It is possible to learn new ways of behaving toward yourself and others. It may take time and effort, but every step brings you closer to the person you want to be. You can create the life you want.

If you always do what you've always done,
You'll always get what you've always got.

Honoring the natural world

Awaken to the divinity beneath your feet and to the divine in the sky that endlessly covers you. BRENDA MALLON

Wherever you are in the world at this moment—on a beach in Greece, in a subway in New York, trekking through a rain forest, sitting at your desk—take the chance to connect with the natural world around you, because this will feed all your senses and can ease the minor irritants of day-to-day living. The traffic jam does not feel so bad when you see the infinity of the sky or the delight on a child's face as she kicks autumn leaves. Explore the synergy of your senses, marvel at how they work together: as you peel an orange recognize the dexterity of your fingers that release the smell and how this prepares your taste buds—the experience of eating an orange can become a work of art, if you let it. Cultivate all your senses, for they feed your imagination and allow you new ways to appreciate the nuances in the world, both inner and outer.

One way to honor the natural world is to be in it fully, and the following exercise will help you do just that.

* Take ten minutes to walk around outside. Use all your senses to record your experience. Feel the temperature of the sun on your skin. Note the distinctive smells of the season. See how the light changes at certain times of the day. Listen

to sounds that surround you, and then listen some more to the elusive sounds that often go unnoticed.

* Imagine you are seeing the world for the first time. Turn over a stone and look at the earth beneath it with a fresh eye. Make a list of any plants, animals, or natural features that catch your attention. My list read as follows: tulips, daffodils, a yew tree, pink clematis, mock orange blossom, drooping hyacinths, slug trails, pigeons flapping.

* Add descriptions: lush leaves, washed streets, dusty evening light, sun-baked stones.

* Write a poem or a letter in praise of what you saw using the feelings that these objects invoked in you and the thoughts they inspire in you.

Embrace your inspiration

Make a habit of carrying a notebook or sketchpad with you. When you find yourself in a place that feels special, soak up the atmosphere and then record it. If you have an idea, note it down for consideration later. Tiny jottings are the seeds that can blossom into well-formed projects. Listen to your inner voice whenever it calls and value it by recording it with one of the following affirmations:

My life is an inspirational journey.

I accept my potential to create the life I want.

I open myself to intuition and wisdom.

Develop a creative dialogue with yourself, bounce ideas around, and ask "what would happen if I put this with that?" If you are rejecting ideas as soon as they arise, recognize the fact, then celebrate the knowledge that your ideas will bloom, given more time and attention. Give your ideas resting space in your notebook and go back to them when you have time.

Cherish the voice that whispers out of the blue.

Crystals for creativity

Precious and semiprecious stones are valued worldwide for their beauty. Many are believed to have intrinsic qualities that enhance healing energy. Carefully chosen crystals placed around the home or person will absorb negativity and improve creative expression. When buying a crystal, clear your mind and choose the one you are intuitively attracted to. Cleanse it in cold running water and then leave it to dry in sun- or moonlight. Place it in your home where the light will fall on it and enhance its color.

Amber Good for bringing calmness and absorbing negative energies. Used by healers as a protection against taking on another person's pain.

Amethyst Known to enhance spirituality and for its healing properties.

Aquamarine Linked to good vision, clarity, and communication.

Bloodstone Absorbs negative energies.

Blue topaz Encourages artistic growth, calms body and mind, and aids concentration.

Holley blue/purple Helps focus vision and clarity on life's purpose. Useful in self-healing.

Orange calcite Improves awareness and self-confidence and increases vitality.

Quartz Energizes and adds strength and insight.

Rose quartz Promotes emotional balance and healing.

Ruby Associated with heat and passion. Improves mental agility.

Sapphire Promotes faith, friendship, and love. Boosts the imagination.

Turquoise Provides protection, increases confidence, and aids intuitive awareness.

Ways to let the imagination speak

Children live in a world ruled by their imaginations. They can transform themselves into monkeys or mermaids and back again in seconds. To them, a table can also be a cave full of monsters, a horse, or a mountain. The responsibilities of adulthood often deaden our imaginations, forcing us to see things literally.

The following exercises teach us to be still and listen to the creative child within us all.

* Center yourself in the present moment. See yourself as still and as timeless as a great rock. Feel the weight of its experience across the ages. Recognize your link with all that has gone before and all that will come in the future.

* Sit quietly. Let your imagination whisper to your waiting self. Be open to any thoughts, words, images, and sensations that come to you.

* Turn off the busy mind censor. The ceaseless "chatter" we usually experience, combined with our tendency to be judgmental, cuts us off from the creative mind. So be gentle with yourself, be as soft as cupped petals that collect the rain that sustains the flower. Let yourself be a vessel to receive intuitive nourishment.

* Let regular events during your day trigger your imagination. As you go through a doorway, which is the symbolic threshold between one place and the next, between one world and the next, stop. What thoughts come to you in your momentary stillness?

Spontaneous joy

It can be a struggle to let go of your "grown-up," sensible persona. Worrying about the impression you make on other people stifles spontaneity, yet you still delight in the free child who splashes in puddles and rocks with laughter. It is time to reclaim your own free spirit. Here are some ideas to help you leave behind your old constraints, go beyond your usual parameters, and urge yourself forward where you would normally hold back. Go with what appeals to you at the moment.

✳ Take yourself less seriously. Laugh if you catch yourself being pompous or too earnest.

✳ Clown around for a while. Learn how to do a magic trick. Even better, learn how to do a magic trick badly.

✳ Make yourself a jester's cap.

✳ Get some face paints and transform yourself into a favorite animal or character.

✳ Delight in the unexpected. If a friend phones up out of the blue, take the day off.

✳ Get a large sheet of paper, bright colors to write with, and set down as many joyous words as you know. Just seeing them written down will make you smile.

✳ Gladden your heart by playing your favorite music. Close the curtains and pretend that you are the lead singer, performer, or conductor.

✳ Dress yourself up in your most glamorous clothes and take yourself out—you're worth it!

✳ Play hopscotch. Never learned? Now's the time to find out.

Intuition: Your inner muse

When we look at the landscape around us we often make intuitive links between what we see and how we feel. Perhaps this is not surprising when we realize that the word intuition derives from the Latin *intueri*, to gaze upon, from *tueri*, to look at. Such insights are not limited to our connection with the natural world, however. In all walks of life we can draw on the instinctive power and knowledge of our intuition. Our inner muse speaks when we are willing to listen.

The following exercises teach us to recognize its voice.

* Turn off external distractions. For a week switch off the television and radio, stop reading newspapers, and let in the sound of creative silence. What you begin to hear is your inner muse. Listen and take note.

* Trust your inner muse. Build up your intuitive wisdom by learning from the inner voice each time it speaks to you. When you give yourself permission to be at peace, you open up to another level of being. You drop from the crowded surface of your conscious mind to a fertile space, deep within your subconscious, where new ideas germinate. You can hear the rustle of thoughts and feelings that were previously drowned out by the chatter of your conscious mind.

* Sit down in front of a mirror. For five minutes observe yourself. Examine your face as if you have never seen it before. What do you see? What does your face tell you about your life? What story does it want to tell? When you've finished looking, draw a picture or write a story titled "My Face."

The sixth sense

We all have an instinctive power of perception known as the sixth sense, which is most apparent in the rich creative world of dreams, prophecies, and superstitions. If properly harnessed, it can add an extra dimension to all that we say and do.

How do you develop your sixth sense? One way is by attuning yourself to listen to your feelings. The next time you have a "hunch" that something is about to happen or that something is wrong with a friend, stop and give yourself time to digest it. What is the feeling communicating? Do you need to act on it? If so, pick up the phone and call your friend. You don't have to be dramatic about it, just say, "You suddenly popped into my mind so I thought I'd give you a ring. How's everything with you?"

There are many reports of people having a sense of danger that has acted as a warning to them. If you experience such a feeling, respond to it and investigate the fear. If your fear is unfounded, at least you will have put your mind at rest. A woman I know had a recurring image of fire. Rather than ignore the image, she thought about what constituted a fire risk in her home, and in the process, had the electric wiring checked. Her sixth sense paid off. The electrician discovered that sheathing on some of the wiring had worn through. He said, "You probably saved your life, this was a fire waiting to happen. You don't know how lucky you are." She didn't tell him it was owing to her sixth sense rather than luck.

Making connections

A moment of inspiration, a sudden flash of knowledge, usually brings with it a burst of energy and pleasure—that "a-ha" moment when all becomes clear. At this point connections are made that were missing earlier. Sometimes these links can disappear again like wisps of smoke, so capture them in your Creative Year Journal as soon as you think of them. Draw or write a message to yourself. These little connections can be expanded and embellished at a later date to become a passage in a story, the message of a painting, or the focal point of a tapestry. In the meantime, however, just celebrate the grace of that moment of inspiration.

If you get inspiration from a book it is probably because the writer connects to your own core. The Irish poet W. B. Yeats is reputed to have said to someone who admired his work, "If what I say resonates with you, it's merely because we are branches of the same tree."

Having faith in yourself brings creative power. Have the courage to follow up the connections you make and pursue clues that offer you new insights. Believe in yourself, trust that your ideas and goals are worthwhile and achievable, and you will succeed.

Meet your authentic self

You can find inspiration in your past, as Sarah Ban Breathnach does in her book *Something More: Excavating Your Authentic Self*. To do so, you need to revisit earlier years. The acronym DICE can be helpful in the following exercise:

Dig down.

Investigate what you have unearthed.

Choose what is of value.

Explore and expand.

Find a comfortable place and give yourself half an hour or longer to take a trip into the past. For some, this may feel frightening, but even if you had a difficult childhood it is possible to find nuggets of rare beauty in the midst of the garbage. The child you were is still in the heart of you and needs to be acknowledged and incorporated into the creative adult you have become.

Take your mind back to when you were seven, eleven, fourteen, or eighteen. You can just do one age now and return to the others at another time.

For each age, ask yourself the following questions. Make some notes in your Creative Year Journal to help you recall later.

* Where did you live?
* Who did you live with?
* What made you happy?
* What made you sad?
* Did you have a special friend or friends?
* What was the high point of your day?
* What was the high point of your week?
* Was there anything happening that made you different from your school friends?
* If a stranger met the child you were at this age, how would they describe you?

Come back to the present and reflect on the following questions:

* What did you learn at that age that is still useful to you today?
* Are there things you used to enjoy then that you could choose to do now?
* Did you unearth anything that surprised you?

If you remembered talents that have become rusty, is it now time to resurrect them and expand your creativity?

Embrace the child you were then, who did the best he could with the knowledge he had then. Celebrate his survival and congratulate yourself for having come so far.

Emotional intelligence

You cannot prevent the birds of sorrow from flying over your head, but you can prevent them from building nests in your hair.
CHINESE PROVERB

Emotional intelligence is the ability to respond to situations and challenges with the emotional response that is most likely to result in a positive outcome. If you moderate a strong first reaction, then unwelcome confrontation can be avoided. For example, if your teenage daughter is late coming home you are likely to fear for her safety. When she walks through the door, this fear is quickly transformed into relief and rage that she worried you so. She could be feeling guilty and perhaps defiant, and a showdown is likely to follow. On the other hand, if you reveal your worry to your daughter and understand her need for privacy and freedom, she is much more likely to let you know where she is and what she is up to in the future.

Reflection is an important part of emotional intelligence. Without it, you will be far less reasonable, both toward yourself and your own feelings, in terms of understanding them, and toward other people, in your reaction to them.

It is easy to see why emotional intelligence is an important attribute for a politician or businesswoman, but surely "creative people" are much more honest with their emotions? This is to see emotional intelligence as a black art used to manipulate the unwary. In fact, being in touch with your emotions and having the ability to recognize similar emotions in others is fundamental to the artist. An eloquent silence can be just as important in a novel as an emotional outburst.

With reflection you can use the following primary emotions to create positive situations in your life and in your creativity:

Anger Sadness Love Fear Enjoyment Surprise Disgust Shame

And there are the mixtures and blends that make up complex emotional responses. Let your emotions be your advisers. Acknowledge them, then sift your response and decide how you want to act. Passions, when they are well respected and exercised, have wisdom. They can lead us to great heights and fulfillment and ensure our survival. Passion unregulated and uncontrolled, in other words managed unintelligently, can lead to destruction of ourselves and others. When you are with other people always bear in mind the fact that you are not dealing with creatures of logic but with creatures of emotion. Use your emotional intelligence to empathize and choose your words and actions positively.

I will speak ill of no man and speak all the good I know of everybody. BENJAMIN FRANKLIN

Taking stock

The term "taking stock" was used in farms and shops to describe the regular counting of raw materials or goods in store. To take stock is to make an inventory or appraisal of prospects and resources. Each month it is valuable for you to look back at what you have written in your Creative Year Journal and consider what you have learned about your creative self. Make space in your life to go though all you have drawn, recorded, photographed, and collected as you completed the activities.

On the left-hand page of a clean double spread write the following statements, then complete them:

* When I answered the questionnaire I discovered . . .

* I am surprised that I . . .

* I found doing . . . really challenging.

* The parts I enjoyed were . . .

* What I have learned about myself this month is . . .

* The inner resources I've discovered are . . .

* I congratulate myself for . . .

* To develop my creativity further I could . . .

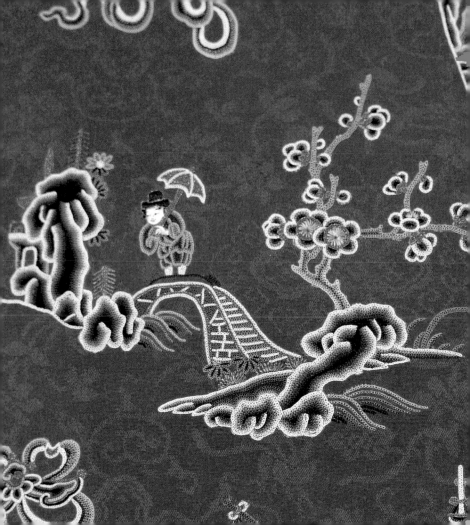

Month 2

Creative Mapping

For thousands of years people have used maps to locate things, to show connections, and to mark sites of special interest. Our emotional and spiritual landscapes, punctuated by events, people, and places, can also be mapped; the resulting increase in self-knowledge can help to power our creative spirits.

This month you will explore your history and the feelings it evokes by making your own maps. You will find out how duality links to intuition and creativity, and discover how the choices we make can open us to our intuitive wisdom or keep us in the straitjacket of cool rationalism, where inspirational insights, and brilliant flashes of understanding are ignored.

We search for patterns in our lives, and discover links between our internal and external worlds. By going to the edges of our experience, the *terra incognito*, the unknown world, we open ourselves to new worlds, places, and people, and can try out unfamiliar ways of behaving. In doing so, we allow deeper layers of ourselves to come forth to meet the challenge of the new. If you are fearful, embrace the sensation; fear sharpens our awareness and causes us to take care. Taking courage and taking care are good traveling companions as we map our world.

The second path

Two is a powerful number—it links us to the dual nature of reality. The tension between and the union of opposites is the creative power that brings movement and change to our lives. It is important in our intuitive awakening because, like the universe, each one of us has these opposites within us, which we can learn to recognize and ultimately unify.

This duality is expressed in the *Tao Te Ching*, the Taoist classic, by the yin-yang symbol. The two sides of the symbol can be seen as light and dark, day and night, divine and mortal, positive and negative, good and evil, or male and female. Each side of the symbol contains within it the seed of the other.

All opposites have dynamic tendencies: day turns into night, life leads to death, white shades into black, good may sink to evil, and evil aspires to good. Inherent in being human is the intuitive awareness that we contain opposites within us. Sometimes this knowledge can make us uncomfortable, but by embracing our entire inner landscape we can contain or harness those darker parts that we, in our fear, deny. Accepting duality is a key step in recognizing the authentic self.

Questionnaire

Before venturing further with our maps and exploration of creative intuition, it is important to take some compass readings to find out where you are now. The following questions look at your life at the moment; how you see yourself. They also highlight any missing pieces to be retrieved on the creative journey ahead.

* What are the high points in your life at present?

* What are the low points?

* Is there any aspect of your life that feels stagnant, like a swamp?

* Are parts of your life running smoothly like a sparkling river?

* Do you have deep roots with family or friends?

* Have some roots been torn out because of storms in your life?

* Can you think of parts of yourself that you keep hidden from friends or family?

* Where or when do you feel on top of the world?

* What words would you use to describe your emotional landscape, for example, rocky, barren, overcast, filled with sunshine?

* How would you describe the path of your life so far?

Feedback

- A good relationship, a fulfilling career, happy children, or a loving home should all be celebrated and appreciated. Or perhaps the high point of your week is a night out with your friends or staying in and watching the latest episode of your favorite sitcom. Whatever you choose, recognize that the reason it means so much to you is because it is fulfilling a basic need.

- Those parts of your life that make you unhappy are the ones most in need of change. Sometimes relatively small things can make a huge difference. If, for example, a lack of control over your life is making you unhappy, then build yourself a timetable and stick to it.

- Stirring up the stagnant areas in your life can be fun! If your job bores you, make a few waves at work and see what happens. Likewise, if your sex life is humdrum or nonexistent, talk to your partner about ways of spicing it up.

- Again, recognize those areas of your life that you perceive as being successful. Can you transfer their success to any other areas of your life?

- Some people are genuine loners, but for most of us the love and support we receive from our family and friends is invaluable. Acknowledge your roots and make sure that you tell those you love how important they are to you. Reciprocate their love and support.

- Family rows, relationship breakdowns, and fights with dear friends cause huge disruption in our lives. Think about those no longer in your life. Does their loss still scar your horizon? If so, is there any way you can rebuild bridges? The death of a loved one is another scar that can be healed only through time and acceptance.

- Dreams, when locked away, die. Paradoxically, those parts of yourself that shame you most flourish in the dark—acknowledge them and see them wither away.

- As we saw in month 1, some places and occasions can be empowering. Cherish them and revisit them as often as you can.

- Our emotional landscapes are constantly changing. If your description is unremittingly bleak, try to think of some fertile, more gentle, or surprising areas of yourself. Likewise, if you see yourself as a safe and pleasant land, try and name a few dangerous areas—rocky cliffs or underground mines—or shaded parts of your life. See yourself as you truly are and how you would like to appear to others.

- Do you see your life so far as a short and pleasant trip or an arduous quest fraught with danger? When you come across obstacles, ask yourself, "Why has the universe put this in my path just now? What can I learn from it?"

Look at your replies and the words you have chosen. How many are negative and how many are positive? What does this tell you about the way you view the world? Think creatively about how you can improve the areas of your life that are making you unhappy. Celebrate all the good things you already recognize.

Making maps to chart personal journeys

It is wisdom to know others; it is enlightenment to know one's self.
TAO TE CHING

One of the ways of seeing where you are on a journey is to look at a map. In the following exercise you pinpoint the physical places of importance in your life so far. In doing so you may jog memories, show boundaries, and discover new connections of significance. Remember that with increased self-knowledge comes increased creativity.

You will need: • A map of your town or city (local hotels or tourist information centers usually carry simple ones that are ideal). If you have moved around the country or world a lot, then you will need a map that encompasses all the places that you have lived in for a significant time. • Colored pencils or felt-tip markers.

And if you want to be a little more adventurous: • Colored paper, tissue paper. • Glue. • Stick-on stars, moons, and so forth. • Ribbons. • Photocopies of photographs of your family, friends, colleagues, pets, and so on.

✳ On your map mark the places that seem most important to you. These could include your place of birth, houses that you have lived in, schools, parks, theaters, churches, and cemeteries. Remember to mark the places that remind you of the bad times as well as the good. It really doesn't matter what you choose. It is your map and if you let your imagination go and let it roam this territory, it will bring you fresh inspiration.

✳ Use whatever materials you have gathered to elaborate your map. Draw and write notes about the events that happened there; add diagrams and stick on photographs or scraps that say something about the place and the meaning it holds for you. There are no rules—trust the process and let your intuition guide you.

✳ Look at your map. In your Creative Year Journal write down anything that strikes you as interesting. Try not to censor your thoughts, just jot down whatever comes into your head. Other people who have created a personal map have written: "I had no idea that places where I used to play as a child were so important. All that feeling of joy and freedom came flooding back." And "When I looked at it I noticed I'd put boxes and frames around nearly everything. I guess it symbolizes my need to control things. I think it's about time I let go. I need to break out!"

Deciding where you want to be

By making our creative desires concrete, we take the first step to making them a reality. The following mind-mapping exercise looks at your desires and helps you to decide where you want to be. It can be used to help you clarify your feelings about relationships, work, or any issue that you are undecided about.

The technique, as designed by Tony Buzan in his book *The Mind Map Book*, harnesses both our cognitive and intuitive sides. By using words, images, numbers, logics, rhythms, colors, and spatial awareness it stimulates all areas of the brain to problem solve and think creatively.

You will need: • A sheet of plain white paper. • A selection of colored pens and highlighters.

✳ Select a topic, problem, or subject to be mind mapped. Turn your sheet of paper on its side (landscape) and draw an image in the center of the page to symbolize the question. For example, if you want to know whether you should move to a new home, then you could draw a house. Use at least three colors in your central image to make it stand out from the page.

✳ Draw thick branches extending from the central topic. On each branch print a key aspect of the topic. For example, important considerations when moving include *money, space,* and *local ties.*

* Now draw thinner lines off the thick branches. Print information on these that are relevant to the key aspects. For example, *extra bedroom* would be a consideration when looking at the *space* issues of a new home.

* Use arrows to make connections between branches on the map.

* Colors and images should be used throughout to highlight themes, emphasize important issues or events, and make the mind map beautiful.

Visioning

Recent studies have shown that we are most likely to reach an objective if we can see it and imagine the steps to reach it. Visioning can be used to reflect the past, to celebrate the present, or to influence the future. This month we are concerned with exploring our life path in order to increase our creative potential. In the following exercise you will create a montage titled *Home Is Where I Start From*. Family, time, money, style, comfort, and security are some of the topics that are connected to the home.

You will need: • A pile of old magazines. • A large sheet of plain paper. • Glue.

* Tear out pictures from your pile of magazines that reflect your home as you see it. Choose images that illustrate your physical and emotional surroundings. Think about colors and furniture. Include pictures of animals if you want to. Don't bother to cut the pictures out with scissors—this is not an exercise in precision.

* Spread the images in the center of your table.

* Build up a composite picture, linking topics or rooms if you wish.

* Glue your pieces on to the sheet of paper once you are satisfied with the arrangement.

* Now, sit back and look at your creation. What do you see? What surprises are there? What flashes of insight? Perhaps your home has a unity, theme, or characteristic that you had never noticed before. Or maybe the different personalities of the people who live there are revealed in their own areas of the house.

* If there is a part of your picture that poses another question or that you would like to develop further, then go ahead and make another picture. You can use visioning whenever you want; there are no limits.

Exploring the liminal

The liminal is the barely perceptible area on the sensory threshold. It is where one part stops and another starts. As you walk along a shoreline after the tide has gone out, you see gifts that the sea has brought to the land. For just a matter of hours you can collect the driftwood and explore the area that will soon go below the water once more. The liminal edges may lead to uncharted territory. In old maps of the world, uncharted areas were often marked "Here, there be dragons" or illustrated by mythical creatures that represented the fear of the unknown.

Throughout the journey of life we often have to enter uncharted waters and face imaginary dragons. We have to go beyond our comfort zone to make new discoveries. For example, one of my clients who had separated from her husband desperately wanted to go on a vacation, but she had never organized a trip or been abroad without her partner. She was filled with worry. "What if my daughter gets ill?" "What if the luggage gets lost?" When I asked what she would do in these situations, she had straightforward solutions. Eventually, she faced her metaphorical dragons, and went on the first of many wonderful trips. One bonus she did not anticipate was a huge boost in confidence, which has transformed her ability to enjoy new experiences in all areas of her life.

In terms of your own creativity, the margins are where the most exciting things can happen. Think about the borders of your life. Are you being hemmed in by a fear of failure, of being laughed at, of being out of your depth? How about work—have you got the opportunity to be creative? Do you take advantage of any training that is offered? Could you explore voluntary work as a way of exploring new avenues? Can you make the most of unexpected opportunities? If you meet someone who is interesting and you exchange contact details, do you follow up your exchange with a note or telephone call? Push back the borders and a whole new world appears.

The two most important qualities we need for our future development in the world of work are enthusiasm and creativity. Adaptability to changing circumstances ensures our survival in all areas of life in a way that habitual responses cannot.

Webs of wonder

The webs that connect people, places, and events, the secrets and coincidences that weave through our lives, can be exploited for their creative potential. Think of the story lines that pivot on a chance meeting, the schools of artists working under a united manifesto, the military leaders taking advantage of political circumstances to seize control: in each situation the author, artist, or soldier has deliberately positioned themselves or their characters for maximum effect.

In the following exercise we physically represent the connections between family, friends, and acquaintances. Some of the connections you will know about already; others will come as a complete surprise. Remember, the web that you are creating will illustrate the interconnectedness of those you know, and can be extended—through the World Wide Web—to link all those on the planet who share your goals and interests.

* On a blank wall or a very large sheet of paper pinned to the wall, write your name and place of origin and the names and places of origin of anyone who lives with you.
* Now, add the details of close family and friends.
* When people visit invite them to add their names and places of origin.
* Use different colors to mark links between people on your web. These can include common friends, relatives, or places.

Ancestral connections

The journeys we make in life are often cyclical. If we look back at experiences we find that themes emerge and that familial patterns abound. Emotional characteristics can be inherited, just like physical attributes. And like our looks, our emotional legacy usually has its strengths and its weaknesses. By laying our ghosts to rest we can free ourselves from some of the restraints on our creative souls.

Look honestly at your life. What are its dominant themes? In relationships are you attracted to a certain type of person? Do you find yourself making the same mistakes over and over? Are you an adventurer or has your fear of change repeatedly stopped you from doing the things that you want? Do you have any addictions that you find impossible to kick? Now consider your parents. Do any of the themes you've identified find an echo in their lives? If you have the necessary information, continue this exercise back through the generations as far as possible.

By thinking about your ancestors' lives and looking for similarities with your own you can bring completion to some of their unresolved fears and uncertainties that have reverberated through the generations. My mother's father was killed in France when she was eight years old. No one in his immediate family had the opportunity to leave Ireland and visit his grave. As part of the completion for my ancestors I will visit his grave and lay a wreath as a tribute to his life.

Properties and places

A place for my heart
My heart at peace
That's what home means.   BRENDA MALLON

Where we live has an enormous effect on our outlook and our creative potential. Some people flourish in a throbbing city, surrounded by people and machines, noise and ideas. Others yearn for the relative isolation of country life, where they have the peace and solitude they need to realize their dreams. The homes map you produce in the following activity helps illustrate where and when you have felt most comfortable in your surroundings.

You will need: • A big piece of paper or card. • A selection of colored pens.

•   Imagine you are taking a journey to all the places you have lived, to each home you have spent time in, and to all the towns and countries you have visited that made an impact on you. Picking a color or colors that you feel reflects its qualities, draw the first home you lived in.

•   Next draw a road that takes you to your next home or special place. The road need not reflect the distance between or direction of your next home, it simply signifies a journey. Draw this home using the colors you feel describe it best.

•   Continue drawing roads and houses until you reach your present abode.

- Look at the finished map. Have you traveled far or do you live in the same town or village that you were born in? Have you always lived in the same type of home? In which homes were you happiest? Where were you less happy? Can you see any pattern emerging about where and how you choose to live? Make notes in your Creative Year Journal.

Patchwork maps and memory boxes

Our memories form a wonderful resource that feeds our creative personalities. The following simple ideas capture important memories in decorative objects. When finished, these objects act as lasting reminders of former times.

✳ Make a traditional patchwork out of scraps of cloth from old clothes or curtains. Sew them together in small squares to create a memory cover. (Depending on your needlework skills and the size of your ragbag, this could be a full-size quilt, a cushion cover, or a small piece that you frame and hang on the wall.)

✳ Gather photographs of your family and friends and create a collage of memories.

✳ Make your own memory box. Collect small items that have particular significance for you. These could be dolls or toys, clothes you wore as a child, a locket, a present from a relative, or a holiday keepsake. When you have assembled your collection, decorate the box. Finally, write a note to someone who might open this box in the future, explaining the significance of its contents.

Body maps

Our bodies are the tools that we use to create. Fingers tap out words on computer keyboards or hold pencils, pens, and paintbrushes. Eyes capture scenes and events for our brains to mull over. Faces and limbs can convey a wealth of expressions. Our organs register excitement, love, hate, and every other emotion that powers our creative souls. This final map illustrates how you feel about your physical body—information that is inextricably linked to your self-confidence and creativity.

You will need: • A sheet of white paper bigger than yourself. • Colored pens, crayons, or paints. • A friend.

* Lie on the paper and ask your friend to draw around you. Once you have the outline, stand up and look at the shape that is before you.
* Think about your body. How hard does it work for you every moment of the day and night?
* Think about parts of your body that are problematic for you—do you have a chronic medical condition or trouble sleeping? Are you unhappy with a physical characteristic?
* With your pens, crayons, or paints color your body. Use abstract patterns or draw animals, birds, stars, planets, and anything else that comes to you.
* Trust the intuitive process. Don't think about what your body map will look like at the end, just fill in what you want where you want.

✳ Get up and walk around your body map. Think about where you started to fill it in and where you finished. Look at the colors and the images you included. Write your thoughts and feelings about how the process felt and what your body map tells you about your self-image in your Creative Year Journal.

The path of love

Nobody has ever measured, even poets, how much the heart can hold. ZELDA FITZGERALD

As I write this, it's Valentine's Day. It was an unusual start to the day—my husband gave me a card he'd made. On the cover it said *7000 Days*—exactly how long we'd been married. Inside he listed significant days, beginning with our wedding day and including the days our children were born, when they started school, and the most amazing millennium party ever! A record of some of the events on our path of love.

Love has many sources: parents and grandparents, siblings and children, partners and friends, even pets. For many, the most important font of love in the universe springs from God. In thinking about the path of love in your life it is helpful to consider what you mean when you use the word. Write the word "love" at the top of a page in your Creative Year Journal. Then underneath it put down any words or phrases that spring to mind. Give yourself at least three minutes to do this.

LOVE

- Care • Kindness • Sex • Compassion • Being thought about • Looked after
- Having fun • Being the most special person • Reciprocal • Needed • Poetry
- Companionship • Going out • Staying in • Cuddling • Massage • Guarded by
someone • Knowing someone will always be there for you, no matter what
- Acceptance • Communication

On your list you may have some negatives such as "Love is not being hurt" or "Love is not being cheated on." If you have got negatives then try to turn these into positives: "Love is being treated with kindness" or "Love is being faithful or monogamous."

In her book *The Measure of My Days* American psychologist Florida Scott-Maxwell questions the contradictions of love, asking "I wonder why love is so often equated with joy, when it is everything else as well—devastation, balm, obsession, granting and receiving excessive value, and losing it again. It is recognition, often, of what you are not, but might be. It sears and heals."

The path of love is the path of the heart. It is what makes us feel alive. It has inspired more creative works than all other human emotions combined. Reflect on the events in your life that made you feel loved, no matter how small or seemingly insignificant.

Taking stock

Look back at what you have written in your Creative Year Journal. Take time to reexamine the collage you made, the maps you drew, and all the notes you recorded as you completed this month's activities.

On the left-hand page of a clean double spread write the following statements:

* When I answered the questionnaire I realized . . .
* I am surprised that I. . .
* I found doing . . . really fulfilling.
* The maps I made told me . . .
* What I have learned about myself this month is . . .
* The inner resources I've discovered are . . .
* I congratulate myself for . . .
* To develop my creativity further I could . . .

Now complete the statements.

On the right-hand page expand your ideas, reflect on your feelings, and consider new places you want to visit, whether physical, spiritual, or emotional. Take the opportunity to recognize the importance of the road you have traveled and value the lessons you have learned on the way.

Month 3
Creative Myth-making

Myths are truths written in symbolic language. They are the old stories that wrap and protect ancient wisdom. Down the generations they tumble, explaining the universe and the human condition. Myths can be a screen onto which we project our deepest emotions. They allow us to step back, take a breath, reflect, and ultimately, move on.

Often we fail to recognize that our own lives are also mythic. This chapter shows you how to explore your story, how to turn the pages from its starting point until you reach the "now" of your tale. As hero of your own myth, you can recognize your qualities of courage, identify the monsters that threaten you, and see the epic voyage you must make.

You will write stories about your life, family, and friends, and in that process discover the guides and heroes in your personal journey toward greater creativity. In addition, you will choose legendary figures, both ancient and modern, fabled and real, to enrich and enhance your life. In exploring myths and making up some of your own you will create fresh ways to make sense of your life and your history.

The third path

The number three is the sign of the Christian trinity: the Father, the Son, and the Holy Ghost. A sacred trinity—Brahma, Vishnu, and Shiva—also dominates the Hindu pantheon. Three symbolizes spiritual synthesis. It represents harmony and a resolution of the conflict of duality. Where there are two elements, a third appears to unify the first two. For the Greek mathematician Pythagoras, three was the perfect number because it signified a beginning, a middle, and an end.

The number three is a common motif in myths, too. Challenges are often given to three brothers, three sisters, or three suitors; heroes may be granted three wishes. Fairy tales require that when words are said in triplicate, magical events come to pass. Hungarian gypsies, at baptisms, would deliberately place three pieces of food on the baby's bed as offerings to appease the three goddesses of fate.

In psychoanalytical terms three represents the id, the ego, and the superego. These three divisions of the psyche were captured in fairy tales long before Freud identified them. In a typical tale a simple boy, who represents the id or basic human drive, would remain true to his nature and follow his instinct, outdoing the greedy and "clever" characters (the ego and the superego) who lose touch with their humanity.

Questionnaire

The aim of these questions is to identify the myths and legends most significant to you. They help to identify those gifts and attributes you yearn for, and those demons that you most fear.

What stories do you remember reading or hearing from your childhood?

※ Which story is the one you like best?

※ Which one was most disturbing?

※ If you could cast yourself in the role of any fairy tale or mythic character who would you choose?

※ Think of your partner or friends. Who would you choose to represent them?

※ If you were given three wishes, what would you choose?

Feedback

• Think about the earliest stories in your life. Can you remember how they made you feel when you heard them for the first time? Are there any themes that link these stories? Children use stories to help them make sense of their surroundings, so your world view will have been shaped in part by these early tales.

- What is it about the story that you chose that made you favor it above all others? Can you see any parallels between this story and the story of your life so far? Tales of courage, of triumph over adversity, of true love conquering all, have inspired generations of children and adults alike.

- Ask yourself the same questions about the story you found most disturbing. The loss of a parent is a common theme in fairy tales, as is cruelty by a wicked stepmother or ogre. These betrayals strike at the heart.

- Did you choose your character because he or she "lived happily ever after," or does he or she have qualities that you desire? If the latter is true, what are they?

- Does the character you chose for your partner or friend share qualities with that person, or is that wishful thinking? If the latter is true, what are the qualities you would choose for the important people in your life?

- Can you make those wishes come true without waiting for the good fairy to turn up?

- Spend some time exploring how you can set about making your dreams come true. This can be a daunting task, especially if you have always been told to stay in your place, not to aim too high. The first step is to allow yourself to imagine what you would like to be or how you would like to live your life. Make simple notes in your Creative Year Journal. Once you set your dreams on paper they enter the concrete world and start to become more of a possibility.

Once upon a time (I)

All fairy tales are set in a distant land and involve characters who have particular functions, though they may not be individually named.

Looking at our lives as a fairy tale helps us to identify the obstacles we have come across, the gifts we have been given, the dreams we hope to obtain, our heroes and villains, loves and hates. It increases our self-knowledge and helps us to recognize familiar archetypes on our journey toward greater creativity.

Beginning with "Once upon a time," write your life as a fairy tale, using some or all of the following characters and symbols:

- Kings and queens—authority figures who stand for parents.

- Princes and princesses—who may symbolize sisters and brothers.

- Wicked witches or wizards—people who have caused you harm.

- Talking animals/magical creatures—the people or guides who have helped you in difficult times.

- Gifts—things you've been given to help and protect you; skills you have learned.

- Task—the task you have had to take on in your family story.

- Conflict—the major problem in your life; the demons you fight (the successful resolution of this is central to the story).

The myth of my birth

Previous events shape our present, whether they are visible characteristics that we carry in our bodily frame or the mythical legacies we have inherited. Look at your own beginning, the facts and stories surrounding your birth. Was it a miracle that you were conceived at all? How did your first days on this earth shape the person you are today?

Record your responses to the following questions in your Creative Year Journal. Don't worry if you do not know the answers to some of the questions, because you have never been told, because you were adopted, or because your parents never spoke of these things. A lack of information need not be a hindrance—it gives you a blank canvas on which to paint your ancestry.

* In what town and country were you born?

* In what town and country were your parents born?

* In what town and country were your grandparents born?

* Do your features and coloring show your links to your ancestors? If so, how?

* Were you named after anyone in particular, such as a relative or famous person?

* What qualities of the past generations live in you today?

* What do you know about your birth?

* What happened immediately before and after your birth?

Naming

Our names are central to our identity. Our first names can reflect the hopes, dreams, and aspirations of our parents or they can link us to a beloved friend or relation. Often ancestral family occupations are revealed in surnames—think of Brewer, Smith, and Thatcher. Each language has its own examples. My family name, Mallon, connects me to a part of Ireland where it is very common, though it is not often found where I live in England. Like many names it reveals my geographical roots. Names can also reflect ethnic origins, cultural roots, religion, and status: Sir John, Lady Helena, Guru Nanak, and President Kennedy are all examples of this last category. They define us to others as an enemy, a friend, "one of us," or "one of them." Names place us in history.

What is your name and what does it say about you? Do you know who named you and why your name was chosen? Does it have a geographical or historical significance? Spend some time finding out about the meanings of your first and family names. Do you think they accurately reflect who you are?

The hero's journey

Stories of heroic journeys are particularly relevant to those on a voyage of creative discovery, because many of the episodes encountered by the hero are also encountered by the artist.

What happens on the hero's journey?

- There is separation, initiation, and return.

- The hero must make the journey even though he might not know where he is going.

- He meets dangers and obstacles block his path.

- He finds willing helpers at critical moments.

- Gifts may be given.

- At last the destination is reached.

- Finally, the hero goes home, changed and enlightened, bringing new wisdom to his community.

In the mythic journey the hero has to let go of the past with all its certainties, its goals, its dogmas and gifts. He has to be prepared to be dead to that world and to be reborn from within. His task is to return to us, transfigured, to teach us the lesson of life renewed; the hero's message is about discovering eternal life.

The hero's first task is to withdraw from the world and go to the regions where deep difficulties of the psyche reside. Here he must clarify the dangers and obstacles, delete them from his history (fight his demons), and then break through to undistorted direct experience—truth!

Many of us experience the heroic journey in dreams, as we will explore later. For now bear in mind any dreams in which you have had to make a journey that contained elements of danger and yet you were compelled to continue—to overcome obstacles, to reach a significant place—even though you did not know what the destination was. These mythical dreams symbolize our personal heroic path.

Rites and rituals

All societies mark the major events in life—birth, naming, puberty, marriage, and burial—with ceremony. These occasions usually take the form of public gatherings, where friends and relations, elders and neighbors congregate to acknowledge that someone is making the transition from one life stage to the next.

Such rites of passage are steeped in tradition. Many rituals are reenactments of society's sacred myths and so may contain symbolic forms or archetypes that communicate directly with our psyche or soul. For example, the water used at a christening is not only symbolic of

Christ's own baptism in the River Jordan but also of the life-giving and cleansing properties treasured by our ancestors through the ages.

Dig out photographs, service sheets, newspaper cuttings, or other material that marks some of these rites of passage for you or your family. Other occasions you may want to consider include first communion, confirmation, Bar Mitzvah, engagement, and degree ceremonies. Think about the events you have attended both as a witness and as a participant. How have these rituals changed your life?

The goddess rediscovered

The oldest religions worshiped the earth as an all-powerful goddess, the ultimate creative symbol. Later societies explained the goddess's many attributes by giving each aspect of her personality a different name. In Ancient Greece, for example, there were seven major goddesses, all with different areas of influence. The names of their Roman counterparts are given in parentheses.

Aphrodite (Venus) Goddess of physical beauty, sexual love, and fertility. Goddess of protection for all women.

Hera (Juno) Goddess of marriage and worldly power; often associated with women at midlife as they prepare for the passage into old age.

Athene (Minerva) Goddess of wisdom and the city, of war for a just cause, and arts for peace. She guides the career woman and anyone involved in education.

Artemis (Diana) Goddess of sports, the outdoor life, the symbolic hunt, and capture. She is the twin sister of Apollo, the Amazon archetype.

Demeter (Ceres) Goddess of the earth and of grain or cereal, lady of the harvest. The basic foods of life and all vegetation are her dominion.

Persephone (Proserpina) Goddess of psychic knowledge and spiritual seeking. She is the one who was trapped in the underworld and saved by her mother's love and persistence. She journeyed through the darkness to emerge renewed.

Hestia (Vesta) Goddess of the hearth and home. She is the "shining goddess" who is symbolized by the living flame, the light of home.

Are all these goddesses reflected in your life and interests, or are some of them missing? Accept these goddess qualities that lie within. Perhaps you wish for the attributes of one of these goddesses that you presently lack. If that is the case, honor that recognition: look at a book on mythology, read about the goddess, collect illustrations, and make a collage. Make visible the attributes you wish to develop; it is the first step toward achieving them.

Modern legends

We have in our midst people who are legends in their own lifetime; people who bring a special quality to all who touch them—who succeed when everyone else would fail. I wonder if you can think of anyone who fits the bill? Perhaps someone you know in your community, at work, or in the neighborhood.

Those who are legends in their own time connect us to universal goodness and unselfishness. They carry the archetype of wisdom and compassion and are fearless in the face of truth and justice. They are the Wise Old Men who assist our heroes through trials and tribulations, who warn them of dangers ahead and heal their almost fatal wounds.

I asked people to nominate the person they saw as a modern legend, a true hero. Here are some of those names: Nelson Mandela, Mother Teresa, Bob Geldof, Mahatma Gandhi, the Dalai Lama, and Dame Cicely Saunders. Who would you choose? What are the characteristics you see in him or her that you admire so much? How have they inspired you in the past? What have you learned from their example that will help you on your creative journey?

Plan for Life by Mother Teresa

People are often unreasonable, illogical, and self-centered.
Forgive them anyway.

If you are kind, people may accuse you of selfish, ulterior motives.
Be kind anyway.

If you are successful, you will win some false friends and some true enemies.
Succeed anyway.

If you are honest and frank, people may cheat you.
Be honest and frank anyway.

What you spend years building, someone may destroy overnight.
Build anyway.

If you find serenity and happiness, people may be jealous.
Be happy anyway.

The good you do today, people will often forget tomorrow.
Do good anyway.

Give the world the best you have, and it may never be enough.
But give the world the best you've got anyway.

You see, in the final analysis, it is all between you and God;
it was never between you and them anyway.

Once upon a time (II)

Every folk tale or fairy tale carries an essential aspect of the human condition, just as every cell carries the print of life. For example, the archetype of the ugly creature shunned by beauty—in "The Frog Prince" or "Beauty and the Beast"—tells us that we can only love if we are loved. That is why they have such universal appeal and why children want to hear them again and again.

As we listen to the tale we know it has a significant message for us, even though we may not know it consciously, for myths speak to our deepest selves. We are drawn to them though we may never be able to explain why. Each contains a germ of power that feeds our psyche. Remember that fairy tales usually end in "happily ever after." This symbolizes the transcendence of the human spirit; life may be harsh and unfair but the true heart can win through and ultimate joy is the reward.

- Choose a fairy tale you like.

- Read it through again or listen to it if it is on tape.

- Ask yourself some questions:

* What do you like about this story?

* What is the main emotion?

* Which character do you most identify with?

Look for the hero inside yourself

Yet always the traces of the past remain inside
Informing, retelling, illuminating my life. PETER KALU

Archetypes are universal themes that speak to our collective unconscious and are found in the dreams, art, literature, and myths of all peoples. In her book *The Hero Within* Carol Pearson identifies six male archetypes.

The **orphan** suffers loss and rejection. His motto is "life is suffering," and he teaches resilience.

The **wanderer** goes on a voyage of self-discovery. His motto is "life is an adventure," and he teaches self-reliance.

The **warrior** has to prove his worth. His motto is "life is a battle," and he teaches courage.

The **altruist** sacrifices himself for others. His motto is "to the greater good," and he shows compassion.

The **innocent** finds happiness and beauty in any situation. His motto is "life is joy," and he teaches faith.

The **magician** uses his wits and intuition to change the world. His motto is "create the world you want," and he teaches power.

Look at the fairy tale you wrote in "Once upon a time (1)." Is the hero of that story, the hero inside yourself, any (or many) of the above archetypes? If so, do you feel that you have learned from the lessons they are there to teach? Even if your childhood was a painful time, your archetypes can help you to accept and value your early experiences.

Creation myths

Throughout history people have been trying to make sense of the world and their existence in it. As we have seen, our earliest ancestors linked the fertility of women with the fertility of the earth, worshiping a great goddess who gave, maintained, and finally took back life. The creative power of the male principle became increasingly important as societies became more patriarchal, until finally many thought of the universe as being the creation of a supreme abstract god.

Creation and creativity are closely linked, for the myths that explain how and why we came to be on earth feed our imaginative cores. Philip Pullman, author of the *His Dark Materials Trilogy,* recognizes the power of myth. Underlying his story is, he says, "a myth of creation and rebellion, of development and strife." He didn't make the myth explicit in the work, but it was important to have it clear in his mind as the backdrop. The myth connects to all those who have relished this trilogy.

• Study the creation myths of the world. Choose one that you find useful in explaining your universe. What is it about this particular myth that attracts you?

Epitaphs

For many of us, our gravestones will have the final word on our lives. Few people write their own epitaph—such sentences are usually the last summing up of a loved one by their nearest and dearest. Epitaphs can reflect a person's interests or beliefs, shed light on his or her personality, or describe how his or her loss has affected those left behind. As such, epitaphs often reveal the dominant archetype in a person's life. The following inscriptions were taken from gravestones in an English church. The first is a variant on the death-rebirth theme. The second inscription speaks of the unnatural loss felt with the death of a child. The third dedication describes the selfless love often associated with mothers.

We all do fade as leaf.

Hannah Wheeldon, died 1851, age twenty-one.

A light is from our household gone
A voice we loved is stilled;
A place is vacant in our home,
Which never can be filled.

Thomas, died 1904, age twenty-one, .

In memory of my dear wife:
She lived for those she loved,
and those she loved remember.

For Hattie, died aged sixty-nine.

This exercise looks at how you see yourself now and in the future, and how you think others may see you. It increases your self-knowledge and encourages you to imagine where your creative journey might finally end. Answer the following questions in your Creative Year Journal:

* What might your epitaph be?
* What would you like it to say?
* What might others say of you?

Are your answers to questions 1 and 2 the same? If not, what changes can you make to your life to make the second answer true? Are you happy with your answer to question 3? If not, what changes can you make to your life so that you are thought of in the way that you wish?

Taking stock

Look through your Creative Year Journal entries for this month. Consider all you have drawn, recorded, photographed, and written.

On the left-hand page of a clean double spread write and complete the following statements:

- The questionnaire showed me that stories I liked were about …

- The fairy tale I wrote revealed …

- I found … really challenging.

- The parts I enjoyed were …

- What I have learned about myself this month is …

- The inner resources I've discovered are …

- I congratulate myself for …

- To develop my creativity further I could …

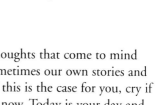

On the right-hand page write down other thoughts that come to mind now you have completed the statements. Sometimes our own stories and those of our ancestors bring great sadness. If this is the case for you, cry if you need to and recognize that you are alive now. Today is your day and in you the hero's journey can continue, armed with increased creativity.

NURTURING

The second phase of your creative journey is a time of blossoming and growth. During this period you may choose to linger outdoors, appreciating the natural world at its most fertile. This is the time to nurture the young shoots of your creative hopes— the fresh opportunities you have made for yourself in your creative journey. During this phase you will complete exercises in Creative Visualization, Creative Enhancement, and Creative Drawing. Each of these brings you a deeper connection to the world and to your unique place in it, and all share the power to nurture and enrich your creativity.

Month 4

Creative Visualization

Creative visualization is a tool that behavior therapists call mental rehearsal. Actors, athletes, and successful corporate executives use it in their work every day. It helps us to gain control over our thoughts, our achievements, and our stress levels. Visualization lets us exercise our imagination. It stimulates our creative ability so that we can make real changes on a physical and emotional level. By honing our imaginative muscle we become more skilled at problem solving and ensure enhanced performance.

Creative visualization is mindfully doing something you do naturally. We all imagine the future, we think about getting ready to go on a visit to friends, we see ourselves making food or talking with others, but most of the time we are unaware of it. In this process we harness the power of the mind through our senses to accomplish a goal.

Creative visualization is positive thinking taken one step further. It is a process of relaxation and focusing in which alpha brainwaves are produced, which is when the most effective communication and reprogramming occurs in the subconscious.

The fourth path

In the number four we find the solidity of the cube and the four sides of a square. For the Chinese, four is the number of the earth, symbolized by the square.

There are four seasons (spring, summer, autumn, and winter), four cardinal points (east, west, north, and south), and four elements (earth, air, wind, and fire). The four quarters of the moon govern the tides of the sea and the tides within people. We are made up of four humors: phlegm, blood, choler, and black bile. When these are in balance we are in "good humor."

In Ancient Egypt, the four sons of the god Horus were guardians of the four directions. Their images were placed in the corners of burial chambers, in canoptic jars, so the souls of the dead would know which way to go on their journey into the underworld.

In Buddhism, the Damba Tree of Life has four branches and the four rivers of Paradise stream from its roots to form a cross.

Christianity has four gospels, four Evangelists, and the four cardinal virtues: prudence, temperance, forbearance, and justice. There are also the four horsemen of the Apocalypse.

Questionnaire

* If you imagine a balloon what do you see?

* If you imagine a lemon what can you taste?

* If you imagine holding a peach what texture can you feel?

* If you imagine an apple what can you smell?

* If you imagine a waterfall what can you hear?

Feedback

• When you use your senses in recollection, as you did in the questionnaire, you are recollecting experiences you have had previously. You do it naturally every day of your life: when you recall an event, when you remember where you left your purse, when you decide what to cook for dinner. Each brings with it a host of sensory associations.

• When you hold a conversation, part of the effective communication involves the unconscious calling up of images and once again, all your senses are involved. As we work through the following guided creative visualization exercises, see yourself as someone in training to develop an important set of sensory and imaginative muscles. You use them all the time but now you are going to bring them to a higher level of performance.

Exploring inner wisdom

To be wise is to use knowledge, experience, understanding, common sense, and insight. In order to learn to be wise people used to, and still do, study the works of great thinkers such as Leonardo da Vinci or read the teachings in philosophical works.

"Wise women" was the original name for witches, who knew of the power of herbs and knew how to use them in healing. Using their skills of observation, they learned which plants were beneficial and which caused ill effects. They took on the role of midwives, helping women to conceive—or prevent conception—and to bring children into the world. They used their inner wisdom, developed over years of taking notice and experimenting, to aid their communities.

• Develop inner wisdom by observing yourself. Note your moods and your performance. When are you at your best? What influences you? Do you react well to deadlines? Do you work better if you pace yourself, making steady progress rather than making sudden leaps? Now look at others in the same intuitive way.

Meeting your guide

Guides go by many names, including companions, guardian angels, and power animals. Guides appear in many places: in dreams, in visions, in visualizations, in meditations, in books that inspire you, and through the mediation of others. They often come at times of extreme distress to show us a safe path, give new direction, and help us succeed when all hope seems gone.

Ernest Shackleton, one of Britain's greatest explorers, met his guide in the most extreme circumstances as he crossed Elephant Island in the Antarctic. In treacherous weather he battled on to find food for his team, who were trapped, left behind in a frozen wilderness. On the journey he felt the presence of a guide, someone who held him safe. Like many others before and since, he hesitated to speak of "the third" who walked beside him, who led him and his three companions to safety in the most dangerous territory known to man. His story inspired the lines in T. S. Eliot's poem "The Waste Land":

Who is the third who walks beside you?
When I count, there are only you and I together
But when I look ahead up the white road
There is always another walking beside you.

- Write down any situation in which you have felt the presence of a guide.

Meeting your power animal

During vision quests shamans visit the territory of power animals. There they meet the one creature who is meant to be their companion, who will empower, guide, teach, and protect them. The power animal shares its natural qualities with the shaman so that he or she can nurture the greater community.

Our power animals roam in dreams; they appear in our visualizations and lurk in the shadows that capture our glance. In the following exercise you identify the power animal that will help you on your creative journey.

✳ Choose an animal or bird that appeals to you now, at this moment.

✳ Visualize it as it moves. Notice its color, the texture of its coat, the sound it makes.

✳ List the qualities of this animal.

✳ What strengths can it offer to you?

✳ See yourself protected and guided by this creature as you go through the rest of your day.

✳ Before you sleep make a note of how it felt to have a power animal by your side.

Flying in light

Light makes it possible for us to see and the sun's illumination lets us see what is going on in our world. When you feel unsure of a course of action, you can use this visualization to see your way ahead and to help you make your decision.

* Visualize yourself in an open landscape such as a newly mown field or a rain-washed plateau.

* See yourself surrounded by the brightest light you can imagine. Let it wash over you, cleansing your mind.

* Let this outer light support you and lift you in flight. Feel your body in radiant air currents.

* Now that you have risen above the pull of gravity, you have a wider view. Consider the decision you have to make. Let ideas flow in this light. Be open to creative ideas.

* Gradually feel yourself return to firm ground.

* Bring your attention back to your special place.

* In your Creative Year Journal write down how you felt and note the decision you made.

The depths of the sea

The sea is often used as a metaphor for our emotional life. Sometimes we feel "all at sea," mixed up and confused, or find ourselves in "heavy seas," where we are buffeted about by turbulence that comes out of nowhere.

* Think of all the associations you can make with the sea. Think of the vastness of oceans, of the Dead Sea and the Red Sea. Consider the life that teems there and the shores that travelers reach with joy and relief.

* Visualize yourself on a boat in a gentle sea.

* Look to the horizon to land that has come into sight.

* See yourself arriving at a place you have longed to visit.

* Take in the aromas, tastes, and sights. Hear the special sounds that define your place. Touch the ground, bless its welcoming solidity after the fluid sea on which you have traveled.

* Make some notes in your Creative Year Journal.

Be kind to yourself

There are no mistakes, no coincidences. All events are blessings given to us to learn from. DR. ELISABETH KÜBLER-ROSS

Often we give ourselves a hard time; we lament our failings and forget to recognize the beauty within. If you are in the habit of putting yourself down, now is the time to take stock. Give yourself permission to be kind to yourself.

In this visualization ask for all the help you need to banish those damaging feelings.

* See yourself in a silk marquee, one of those huge tents that are hired for parties.
* Visualize yourself dressed in purple clothes and surrounded by rich rays of pink and mauve.
* Imagine that your negative thoughts are words written on ribbons attached to your beautiful clothes.
* As you sit bathed in this empowering light see the ribbons becoming loosened. Watch as, one by one, they float away out through the sheer silk of the canopy.
* Visualize the ribbons dissolving into the scintillating blue sky.
* Repeat this visualization whenever you are plagued by negative thoughts and you will strengthen your ability to release hindrances to your well-being.

Accepting your exclusive gift

This visualization is to explore personal treasures that may come in any form.

✳ Imagine you are traveling to a bright clearing next to a river. When you arrive, allow your gaze to move with the flow of the river, taking in all its many changes.

✳ There, at the bend in the river, you see a well with a small roof above it and a bucket resting on the wall that surrounds the water hole.

✳ Go toward the well. When you reach it, notice the contents of the bucket. It contains a box with your name on it. This is a gift for you to help you on your journey through life.

✳ Your whole being is tingling with energy, pulsing with vital life force. Open the box with your exclusive gift and examine it.

✳ Say your thanks to whoever might have given you this present and make your way back to your special place.

Consider what you were given in this visualization. Perhaps it does not feel like a gift but something ordinary. Whatever the gift is, its importance to you at this point is certain.

Reflect on your gift and the journey. Make some notes in your Creative Year Journal and think about what this gift signifies. Remember that it came from your inner wisdom and carries important insights for you.

Wrap yourself in radiance

Look though a prism and you will see that everything in the world is surrounded by color. These colors delight us, heal us, and give us the opportunity to decorate ourselves and our homes. Rainbows, which reveal all the colors of the visible spectrum, are heaven sent.

Traditionally, the rainbow is regarded as the celestial bridge over which gods may walk while men go beneath—a link between the unseen world of the spirit and the seen material world of every life.

* Visualize rainbows you have seen: the shiny rainbows in bubbles, in water puddles, on tarmac roads, and on wet windowpanes.
* Focus on their wonderful hues and let yourself delight in the joy they bring.
* Visualize yourself as a child when you saw a rainbow. Can you recapture the surge of happiness that flashed through your little body? Cherish that connection with delight and breathe in the rainbow.

The rainbow—sign of hope, bringer of wonder to every place it touches, no matter how poor or damaged—is a small piece of magic that illuminates our world.

Symbols of significance

Symbols are part of our world language. They hold a profound, simple wisdom that comes to us unbidden every day of our lives, no matter where we live or what we do. They represent or stand for something else, something more. Think of a dove, for example, the symbol of peace, or the plus sign, which signifies addition.

Many symbols are centuries old. In *The Woman's Dictionary of Symbols and Sacred Objects,* Barbara Walker shows how symbols have personal and universal significance. Their meaning may change over time; the swastika, for example, in Oriental traditions symbolized peace and creativity and was linked to the sun wheel. In the West it became debased so that now it symbolizes cruelty and totalitarianism.

Symbols connect us to the web of humanity that stretches from the past to the future, from the individual to the transpersonal. They tap into archetypal images carried deep within our minds and the visual stimuli of the symbols that surround us and affect us emotionally and spiritually.

✳ Make some sketches of symbols that are used in your area. Look at shops, places of worship, advertising billboards, in restaurants and in magazines. Make a note of what the symbol brings to mind and ask yourself why it was chosen.

✳ Sensitize yourself to the symbols that surround you in your waking life and in your dreams.

Plant the seeds of success

Paul Binding wrote about the power of seeds to survive. In September 1940, London's Natural History Museum was hit in an air raid. Fire-fighters poured water on the precious collections, unwittingly activating silk-tree seeds that had been brought back from China in the late eighteenth century. Some fifty-five years later in China, scientists germinated seeds from 1,200-year-old lotus trees.

In the following visualization you plant the seeds of a project in your mind and wait for them to germinate.

* Think of your project as a plant. What kind of seed would it be? Big like a coconut or with wings like a sycamore seed?

* Imagine planting your seed. What nutrients does it need? The covering of dark compost or an open-air café where it will be stimulated to grow by contact with lots of people?

* Once you have planted the seed you have to let it rest until germination takes place. Be patient.

Improving performance

Creative visualization is a mental process whereby an individual establishes a goal and then imagines the process of attaining that goal. When someone regularly imagines achieving a goal, he or she actually changes. The mind absorbs the subliminal messages and the individual then changes his or her identity in response to the dictates of the subconscious.

This is a visualization to help you achieve your goals, whatever they may be. Study yourself and think about what goal you want to achieve. Bear in mind your strengths and challenges. If you lack skills in languages it is probably not helpful to imagine yourself as a translator. Play to your strengths and choose your goal. Drifting is better left to flotsam unless you have decided to drift as a form of relaxation.

* Imagine yourself achieving your goal.
* Hold a picture of yourself, long and steady.
* Hold the image in your mind's eye. Heighten your senses of smell, taste, touch, sight, and hearing. Include all of these as you see yourself achieving your goal.
* Accept that by visualizing your success you draw it closer to you.

Taking Stock

It is time to make an appraisal of this month's recordings in your Creative Year Journal.

On the left-hand page of a clean double spread write the following statements:

✳ When I completed the questionnaire I found visualizing the objects …

✳ Meeting my power animal was …

✳ I found doing … really challenging.

✳ I enjoyed …

✳ What I have learned about myself this month is …

✳ The inner resources I've discovered are …

✳ I feel the visualizations have …

✳ To develop my creativity further I could …

Now complete the statements.

On the right-hand page expand your ideas if you want to. Remember, you can do these visualizations at any point and you can repeat them whenever you feel they would help you on your creative journey. If you have enjoyed this month's work, my book *Creative Visualization with Color* provides many more guided visualizations.

Month 5
Creative Enhancement

To begin again, to take up life once more, to reenchant your life, can be a challenge, especially after a period of trauma or when you are feeling exhausted. This month you will discover how to flood fresh energy into mind, body, and spirit and build a sustainable bank of creative resources that you can access whenever you need a boost.

Creativity is holding on to something that starts when we are babies. According to D. W. Winnicott, the famous British psychoanalyst, the infant has "the ability to create the world." This sight of the universe as new every time, full of fresh experiences and a sense of wonder, is what the creative soul delights in. To truly enhance every minute of your life, look at the world anew and enrich your sensory awareness by savoring everything.

Paring down an experience can encourage its enhancement—less can mean more. The Chinese philosopher Lao-tzu said that "Pots are formed of clay. But the empty space within is the essence of the pot." This month we learn to appreciate the importance of space, emptiness, and the power of silence to the creative spirit.

The fifth path

The five senses guide our lives. The Law of Five Elements is based on wood, fire, earth, metal, and water linked with the Taoist five seasons of spring, summer, late summer, autumn, and winter.

In the east there are five elements: earth, air, wind, fire, and space. Five is the number of man with arms and legs outstretched to form a pentagon. Like a circle, the pentagon is unending and so it symbolizes perfection and wholeness.

In the Islamic faith there are the five pillars of wisdom, five divine presences, five prayer times during the day. In Buddhism, the heart is said to have four directions, which when you include its center make five and symbolize universality.

Questionnaire

✴ Have you got fresh flowers in your home?

    ✴ Have you got any pictures hanging on your walls?

      ✴ Have you got any photographs in your room?

      ✴ Are you wearing colors that delight you?

      ✴ Can you smell your favorite perfume?

    ✴ Have you got an inspirational book by your bed?

      ✴ Have you listened to any special music in the last twenty-four hours?

  ✴ How long is it since you went for a walk in the countryside or by the sea?

   ✴ When was the last time you prepared yourself some special food?

✴ Are the clothes you are wearing comfortable and pleasing to you?

Feedback

• Fresh flowers fill our homes with scent and color, pleasing the nose and pleasing the eye. They remind us that we too are part of the natural world.

• The artistic work of others can inspire our own creative urges.

• Photographs remind us of loved ones and good times. They bring a smile to our lips and our hearts.

• As we will see in Month 7, color has the power to change our mood.

• Humans are very sensitive to smell. We use perfumes to calm or arouse us.

- When searching for inner wisdom it is important to read and understand the wisdom of others.

- Sound, like light, has a powerful effect on our emotions. Use music to evoke a certain time, place, or person, or simply to relieve tension and lift your mood.

- A closer association with the natural world can offer us healing and stimulate all of our senses.

- Good food not only nourishes our bodies, it feeds our souls. Make sure that you take pleasure in your food. Stimulate your eyes and your taste buds with colorful, delicious foods.

- The clothes that we wear reflect how we see ourselves. Make sure that you are happy with the way you look on the outside—inner confidence will follow.

If you look back at your answers and find that you are not surrounding yourself with the sights, smells, tastes, and memories that are significant to you, then your life is diminished. You are not cherishing the things that feed your senses, soul, and spirit. In Creative Enhancement you will discover how to increase your physical, emotional, and spiritual life and enjoy the process as you do so.

Reenchanting your life

Bringing the five elements into your home helps to add balance to your life.

Wood—Collect driftwood. Find fallen branches on which to hang handmade decorations. Polish any wooden furniture you have or feed it with nourishing oils.

Water—Each day when you wake, pour yourself a glass of water. Drink half and pour the other half onto a plant or onto a garden. This act of sharing affirms your link with nature. The water that you must have to survive is also what all life needs.

Earth—Bring this element into your life by having plants growing in your home or in an outside space. Grow herbs on a windowsill if you are short of space. If you grow things that you can eat you draw closer to that which sustains you.

Fire—Rejoice in the power of fire: burn incense, light candles, or use Native American smudge sticks in purifying rituals that coat your hair and skin with the smell of burned sage.

Metal—Polish metal so that it gleams and reflects the light in and around your home. Use metal to bring you sharp thinking and strength. Like metal, you can move from molten to defined.

Clearing out the cobwebs

Clearing out the cobwebs is a metaphor for getting rid of unnecessary things in your life. What are the cobwebs in your life? Have you developed habits that you are eager to get rid of? Are there changes in your physical appearance that you desire but fail to do anything about? As with the cobwebs in your home, the first thing is to look in the dark, undisturbed places and ask yourself, "Do I want this in my life now?"

❊ Make a list of "cobwebs" you need to clear.

❊ Write this list as a set of goals.

❊ Set a realistic date for when you can start and complete your goals and put these dates in your diary.

Create the life you love

Take yourself and your Creative Year Journal to a quiet place and give yourself an hour of your valuable time. Consider the life you live at the moment. What is going well? What is causing you concern? If you could change things, what would they be? If you could do anything at all, what would you do? Look at your list. Have you wished for things that are outside your power of influence, or virtually impossible to achieve?

For example, when Helen did this exercise she said she wanted to get back together with her former husband who had remarried two years previously. She had tried everything to get him to come back—used her children as bargaining tools, threatened to commit suicide—but no amount of emotional manipulation would make him change his mind. It was hard for Helen to accept that she had no power to bring him home. Instead, she realized that to recover her life, she had to let go. She worked toward changing her life so that she was not focused on reclaiming the past but in making her future. She accepted that she only had the power to achieve certain changes.

A shrine to celebrate

On a path to the fort above the Cretan town of Loutro is a shrine. It contains a small bottle of olive oil to use in the votive lamp, candles, and icons of Greek orthodox saints. Today, there is a garland of geraniums and bougainvillea draped around the outside of the shrine. It is a mark of celebration for some member of this small fishing community, and a place to go to seek solace and guidance.

In many societies people have shrines in their houses in praise of their gods or as a focus for prayer. In the following exercise you decide on the things that bring blessings to your home.

✳ Choose a place with a flat surface that you can leave undisturbed—a shelf, the corner of a cupboard, or a tray on a window ledge; size does not matter.

✻ Consider what you want to celebrate or what enhances your life. Then place any items that have significance for you on this surface. Add and remove things from your shrine when their freshness has faded or when they are no longer important to you. This is a shrine for enhancing and celebrating life and it can include whatever you want it to include.

A friend has assembled her shrine on top of a bookcase. It has a photograph of her partner and their son, shells from her birthplace in Australia, some beads from India after a trip to meet her yoga master, a fresh flower, and some incense. These items change and she regularly lights a small tea candle to honor the life she has.

Being present in the moment

The current moment is our only point of certainty in an uncertain world. Take this moment to listen to the sounds around you, feel the world through your skin, and open your eyes and draw in your world.

Too often we deny ourselves the physical or emotional space to appreciate the elemental forces in our lives. For the next few minutes choose one element and immerse yourself in it. For example, sit by a fire or light a candle and focus on it alone—feel its warmth, smell it, let your mind dwell in its power. When we do this we close down the "oughts" and "shoulds" of the past and future and exist in the moment.

The scent of hope

Hope is a dream of a waking man.   PLINY THE ELDER

If you can allow yourself to learn from your life experiences you will be enriched beyond measure. No matter how "bad" an event is, it has something to teach you. Many people with life-threatening illnesses speak of the "gift" the illness brought. They choose to embrace life in a way that seemed impossible before.

Hope is what keeps us going in the toughest of times. When we actively practice being positive, we keep hope alive. This positive attitude affects our immune system, as the science of psychoneuroimmunology demonstrates. If we allow ourselves to dwell on the misfortunes of our lives, the negative emotions influence the neural networks of our body which in turn depresses the immune system so we are less able to fight off illness or recover when we have been sick. In her book *Molecules of Emotion* Candace Pert explains how this happens. If you are going through hard times, think of other times when you thought you would not survive but you did. Think of people who have survived against all odds. Read about heroic achievements. Fill the well of despair with images of people who inspire you.

• Choose a fragrance that you love. Let that be your scent of hope and smell it to remind you that life still has its miracles.

Cherishing your friends

This friendship circle will help you focus on important people in your life.

✳ Draw a circle, about four inches in circumference, in the middle of a sheet of paper.

✳ Inside the circle write your name.

✳ Now think about your friends and family and how emotionally close they are to you. Add their names in the space around your name. The one you feel closest to will be nearest to your own name, those who were close at one time but are not any longer will be farther away.

✳ When you have written all the names, think about the last time you were together and what you enjoyed about your time together.

✳ Write a card to any friends who you want to cherish. Tell each of them why you are glad to have them as a friend and what you enjoy about being with them.

✳ Send the cards.

Renewal and growth

The act of creating is just as essential a part of our life as eating and breathing. It is also a cyclic process. In the process, during the highs and lows, the light and the dark times, it is important to find times of quiet to reflect on what is happening for you. Silence is as vital a part of creativity as is "doing." In times of solitude, your inner muse is nourished. May Sarton, author of *On Becoming an Artist,* found that her quiet times in her garden nourished her painting and writing.

Answer the following questions in your Creative Year Journal:

* Where is your place of renewal?
* What gladdens your spirit when you are exhausted?
* When were the most important times of growth for your creative self?

Stability zones

When life is in uproar, when you feel stressed and frenetic, you need your stability zones. These are the parts of your life that give you comfort. They provide a place of calm and pleasure when storms rage, and they remain with you when life is going well. They can be people, places, objects, or activities—anything, in fact, that works for you. Others have listed the following as their stability zone: taking the dog for a walk, having a bath with lots of lavender oil and aromatic candles instead of electric lights, cleaning out the kitchen cupboards, listening to music, reading, lying on the sofa eating chocolate, being with a partner, looking through old photographs, having a massage, and being with friends.

- Make a note of three stability zones in your life. Remember to invest time in their upkeep so that when you need them they will be waiting for you.

Taking stock

Look at what you have written this month. Look around your room—have your thoughts on creative enhancement changed it in any way?

On the left-hand page of a clean double spread write the following:

* When I answered the questionnaire I realized . . .
* I am pleased that I . . .
* I found the idea of making a shrine . . .
* The friendship circle helped me to . . .
* What I have learned about myself this month is . . .
* The inner resources I've discovered are . . .
* I congratulate myself for . . .
* To develop my creativity further I could . . .

Now complete the statements.

On the right-hand page expand your thoughts about enhancing your life. Think about what you have written and the changes you have made. You may have come to a deeper understanding about the ways you can enrich your life. Remember, when you reenhance your own life, everyone who comes into contact with you shares a part of that gift.

Month 6

Creative Drawing

You can connect to your natural creativity through drawing and color. Making art in any form is about making connections with your inner world as well as with the wider world around you. Many of us, however, have been taught that we are not artistic, that we cannot make good pictures or produce beautiful paintings. The truth is, we can all draw; artistic brilliance belongs to us all, not just to a few rare souls.

Symbolic thought, as represented by art, may be our oldest heritage. Archaeologists' findings show that our earliest ancestors painted walls and carved bone and stones. They intuitively symbolized their world.

Your creative journey is about to take you into the world where visions are put on paper. For some this will be a daunting challenge, but have faith—true artistry is about seeing the world with an open heart; drawing ability only plays a small part in the making of beautiful pictures.

The sixth path

Six is the number associated with sexuality since it was sacred to the Greek goddess Aphrodite. The flower of Aphrodite is made up of six vesicae with six points. It held magical properties for women in Arabia and North Africa, especially mothers and mothers-to-be, who would wear an amulet to invoke the goddess's protection.

Early Christians called six the number of sin, because it was associated with things feminine and had sexual connections. In contrast, the celebrated mathematician Pythagoras called six the "The Mother."

Questionnaire

✳ Are you sensitive to colors that go together or colors that clash?

✳ Do you enjoy touching different textures?

✳ Can you become engrossed in looking at a landscape or a flower?

✳ If you look at clouds can you see faces, people, or animals?

✳ Can you think of any artists or illustrators that you like?

✳ What do you remember about drawing pictures as a child?

✳ Can you recall any comments teachers or parents made about your artwork?

Feedback

• The first five questions relate to your sensitivity to your environment and your reaction to the visible world. Whatever your answers, the exercises that follow will heighten all your senses and improve your ability to "see" and interpret what you have observed.

• Do your answers to the last two questions reflect feelings of inadequacy? Many of us had childhood experiences that undermined us. Our confidence in our ability to express what we feel and depict what we see is so threatened that we don't even try anymore, believing that we can't draw a straight line.

• In order to overcome this lack of confidence we need to recognize that we are all artists. Every one of us has ability to draw, paint, or sculpt; all we need is the opportunity to try again in an accepting atmosphere rather than a judgmental one. In Creative Drawing you will learn how to set your inner artist free.

The Zen approach to drawing

Drawing as meditation is the Zen approach. It is a way of seeing that puts us in touch with ourselves and takes us to the heart of what it is to be alive. For the following exercise you will need a pencil and paper.

* Find yourself a space, sit, and look around. Let your eyes rest on an object in front of you. Now close your eyes for five minutes and think about the object you were looking at. Open your eyes. Look at the object and feel as if it is looking back at you. Look at it as if it is the most important thing in the world.

* Now take your pencil, hold it loosely, and place its tip on your paper. Looking at your chosen object, and without taking your pencil off the paper, let the pencil mark what your eyes see. Don't look at the paper, look at the object. Follow the journey your eye makes. Don't check what is happening on the paper; the idea here is to really see. The exercise is not about making a pretty picture, it is about becoming one with what it is you are drawing. Let your eye caress the shapes and textures. Don't worry if you go off the paper, just start again in another spot. This undivided attention becomes a meditation and renews your connection to the infinite.

* Look at what you have drawn. It is original because it captures the origins of what you truly saw.

The wise eye

The eye with which I see God, is the same eye with which God sees me.

MEISTER ECKHART

The eye is the mirror of the soul, the lens through which we view life. When we look with the wise eye, "in-sight" breaks through to bring new wisdom. With your eye you hold the whole world; your vision encompasses the universe—each time you look the miracle of creation is there for you to see.

✳ Choose an object and look at it carefully.

✳ Write down what you see, completing these statements:

   • This object is . . . color.

   • This texture of this object is . . .

   • This object is unusual because . . .

   • This object reminds me of . . .

   • This object feels . . .

✳ Now do a drawing that reflects what you have written. See how the process of looking with the wise eye that sees below the surface takes you to a deeper understanding of your object.

Your hands

Enriching vision entails looking with the heart, eye, skin, lips, and every atom of your body. It involves looking anew at the familiar, in this case, your hands.

✳ Place your hands, palms up, on a flat surface. Follow the lines to the interlacing webs around your fingers.

✳ See the shape of your fingertips.

✳ Notice how one hand is different from the other.

✳ Now look at the backs of your hands.

✳ Think about all the people and places your hands have touched.

✳ Imagine the stories they could tell.

✳ In your Creative Year Journal write down any words that describe the life of your hands. Here are some to start with: stroked, slapped, pinched, patted, comforted.

Becoming one

Intuitively we know we must create. Somehow, in some way, we just have to bring something new into the world in which we live. We share that knowledge, so often unspoken, with our ancestors, the first people who lived on earth.

Scientific research shows that early humans were making representations of human life some 220,000 years ago. One of the earliest known images of a woman comes from the Golan Heights on Israel's border with Syria. Its creator chipped away at the volcanic rock to produce her neck, arms, and breasts, flattening the base of the stone to ensure she could stand up.

Just as that sculptor honored a woman by making an image, so you too can honor your world. Honor the small processes, the flashes of inspiration, the glimpses of brilliance in people and plants, the shapes and patterns that surround you in cars and trains or in the streets where you walk. Recognize your human connection with all other beings that live and die as we do.

✳ Find a piece of wood or soft stone—chalk or soapstone are good—and carve a figure to honor your unique being.

✳ Carve it with love and compassion.

✳ Keep it safe.

Images speak

Images speak of our inner nature, which needs to be nourished, delighted in, and given room to blossom if we are to feel balanced and complete. If you feel that part of yourself is missing and you don't know why, it may be that your creative streak has been stifled. To let it sing, you need to play. Try some of the following activities:

* Doodle.

* Splash paint on a large sheet of paper.

* Drop colored inks on paper, then use a drinking straw to blow the ink around.

* Dip a two-inch paintbrush into your favorite color and paint a picture with your eyes closed.

* Using your nondominant hand, paint a shape, then six lines and six splodges. Now, with your dominant hand and other colors complete your picture.

Look at the images you played into being. Let them float in your imagination. Enjoy the fact that they are now free in the world.

Letting a line sing

The artist Paul Klee loved to "go for a walk with a line." His original imagination gave rise to some of the most exuberant paintings of the twentieth century.

✳ Using a pen with black ink or a B graphite pencil imagine you are taking a line for a walk.

✳ Take it to the beach, the café, up a tree, and down a valley before bringing it home again.

✳ On a fresh sheet of paper take your new line to the cinema, the ice-cream parlor, and the opera—let it sing with the chorus.

✳ Look at the drawings you have made. Are the lines singing? If not, maybe you could take them to other places where the music is more to your taste.

Trust the process

Being an artist means, not reckoning and counting, but ripening like the tree that does not force its sap and stands confident in the storms of spring without fear that after them may come no summer. It does come. But only to the patient, who are there as though eternity lay before them, so unconcernedly still and whole.
RAINER MARIA RILKE

Make time to sketch from nature. The act of recording images reinforces your creative self. It is the planting of small seeds, which will germinate when the time is ripe. Such preparations are the equivalent of digging over the earth before crops are sown and pay dividends at harvest time.

Letting go of perfection

Accepting impermanence helps us to let go of perfectionist streaks that cripple creativity. The artist Andy Goldsworthy creates sculptures with leaves, stones, water, snow, and a host of natural materials. These are made outside and part of their beauty is that they respond to their environment and are changed by it. He takes a photograph to mark the piece before it disappears.

This outdoor exercise will help you embrace the beauty of impermanence.

* Gather a pile of stones, pebbles, and rocks and arrange them in a form that pleases your senses. Take a photo or make a sketch. The next day go back and record any changes. Do this over six days and notice how nature has added her creativity to your creation.

* Collect twigs, leaves, and grasses. Weave them together to make a mat. Place your piece on water—a pool, a stream, or in a bowl. Watch as your piece soaks up the element in which it floats; witness its journey. Celebrate the moment of creation and the power of impermanence. When you leave, remember that the process will continue.

Art as medicine

Drawing and painting help us to make sense of life and to understand our feelings. Art therapy is used throughout the world to release painful emotions and to communicate what cannot be said in words.

The link between thwarted creativity and depression is examined in detail in physician Philip Sandblom's book *Creativity and Disease*. He verifies the fact that people who are stressed, physically ill, or mentally troubled feel better when they find creative outlets.

If you are troubled, pick up your paints or pens and draw a picture of your feelings or your situation. You don't need to explain the image to another person—it is completely for you. It will act as a catharsis.

Taking stock

Artistic pursuits help us develop skills of imagination, observation, problem solving, and sensitivity. They also promote mental well-being.

Look back at what you have written this month in your Creative Year Journal. Make space in your life to look at the pictures and sculpture you have produced while completing your creative activities.

On the left-hand page of a clean double spread write the following statements:

✳ When I answered the questionnaire I . . .

✳ I found the Zen approach to drawing . . .

✳ Now when I look at my hands I . . .

✳ What I have learned about myself this month is . . .

✳ The inner resources I've discovered are . . .

✳ I am pleased I . . .

✳ The images that I made are now . . .

✳ The way I feel about perfection is . . .

✳ What I would like to concentrate on is . . .

Now complete the statements.

On the right-hand page expand on your feelings about the creative process. Looking back at the images you made and the words that you wrote, what do you discover about your capacity to be accepting of yourself and your creations? If you find it difficult, perhaps you are seeing through someone else's eyes, thinking how someone else would judge you. The truth is, we discover our artistic souls when we stop trying to conform to other peoples' expectations. When we stop seeking the approval of others, we come into our own. We blossom because we accept who we are.

Some of the most amazing art I have seen is "Outsider Art." Although the artists are all untrained, many have experienced severe mental distress and have created unique pieces for themselves, not to sell or show, but simply because the act of creation eased their lives. Have a look at the Raw Vision website, www.rawvision.com, and perhaps you will give yourself more freedom to be the artist you are.

HARVESTING

Now that we are halfway through our creative
journey, it is time to harvest the crops we have
sown and nurtured in the first and second stages.
In Creative Color, Creative Abundance, and
Creative Writing we use our growing self-
knowledge and belief to try new and exciting tasks.
Take time to appreciate the glory of this stage of
your journey. You are a child of this universe and
can enjoy the fruits of the earth.

Month 7

Creative Color

From the beginning of time, people have intuitively known that color has power. Our early ancestors used natural pigments to color their skins and clothes. Ancient civilizations recognized color as a manifestation of light and linked it to their gods. Priests in Egyptian temples, for example, wore blue chest plates—blue being a sacred color—to show that the gods sanctified their judgments.

In the Middle Ages color was an essential part of heraldry. White symbolized faith and purity, gold stood for honor, red meant courage and zeal, and blue expressed purity and sincerity. Those whose color was black revealed grief and penitence, while green meant youth and fertility, orange showed strength and endurance, and princely purple was reserved for those of royalty and high birth.

We are each bathed in light that we see as color. Color is light made visible. Each color has its own vibrational wavelength, which affects us deeply, both physically and emotionally. As you discover these color properties, you will learn how to expand your creativity through the power of color.

The seventh path

Seven is a mystic or sacred number. It is the sum of four and three: numbers viewed by Pythagoreans and Ancient Egyptians alike as lucky, so in this seventh month of your year of creativity think about all the good things that have come into your life.

There are seven deadly sins: pride, avarice, wrath, envy, gluttony, lust, and sloth; and seven virtues: faith, hope, charity, prudence, fortitude, justice, and temperance. In the Christian faith there are seven gifts of the Holy Ghost, and Christ spoke seven times from the Cross.

We have divided time into sevens: there are seven days in a week, we talk of the seven ages of man, and there are seven phases of the moon. Early astrologers and alchemists recognized seven planets: Jupiter, Saturn, Mars, the Sun, Venus, Mercury, and the Moon, each having its own "heaven."

Questionnaire

✳ What are your two favorite colors? What is your least favorite color?

✳ Look in your wardrobe. What is the predominant color?

✳ Which color have you chosen for major home furnishings?

✳ Think back to when you were a child. What was the color of the dress or shirt you liked best?

✳ If you were a color what would you choose to be?

Feedback

• The colors you like and dislike say a lot about you. As we go through the exercises in this chapter you will discover the properties of each color in terms of its warmth or coolness and symbolic connections. At this stage, just think about the links you make now. Are your favorite colors somber and retiring? Are your least favorites "shout" colors that draw attention and make you feel too visible?

• Many times we have our favorite colors but never wear them or use them in our homes. Do you? If not, why not? Is it fashion that dictates or the opinion of family or is it timidity? Whatever the reason, it is important to recognize that color really does color your life and it's okay to choose the ones that matter to you.

• The colors you choose for furnishings can indicate the mood you want at home. Cool creams bring calmness, deep magentas bring elegance and comfort, and gold brings sumptuousness. Think about whether you are creating the mood you want in your home, room by room.

• A clue to important colors is to return to those you loved as a child. How did they make you feel? Remember those sensations now—jot them down—they will be useful as we work through our rainbow.

• Did you choose a bright "look-at-me" color, or a more subdued one that is more likely to blend into the background? Does this color reflect your personality, the person you are—or want to be?

Color influences us because each color affects the brain differently; each one sends out vibrations that we cannot see with the naked eye. When a color hits our eyes, the signal is transmitted to a specific part of the brain. Different colors hit different parts. Very bright, intense hues and shiny or glittery ones hit the deepest and most primitive part of the brain—the emotional center concerned with hunger, sex, and basic emotions. Think about the effect colors have on you. Do you "see red" when you are angry or feel "a red mist" when you are furious?

Color Therapy

Throughout history, color has been used therapeutically as well as creatively. Scientific investigation has shown us that all matter is energy and all energy is vibration. Each color of the spectrum has its own vibrational frequency and by directing color vibrations we can maintain or change the vibrations of the body to a frequency that gives us health and harmony. This means we can use color to improve our mood and we can choose colors to influence the way other people feel about us.

Most of the electromagnetic energy spectrum is invisible to the naked eye. It ranges from the longest energy waves (radio, television, and radar), through shorter infrared rays, to the shortest waves, the cosmic rays. You may have experienced the healing use of electromagnetic energy in X rays and radium treatment. The visible rays—the eight colors of the spectrum—also have healing powers. Color therapists use colored lights and filters to focus on different parts of the body to bring about release from pain or to induce feelings of relaxation. They also use gems and semi-precious stones to change the energy in the body or in a room. As you explore the potential of the colors in this section keep in mind their therapeutic potential.

White wonders

The snow goose does not need to bathe to make itself white.
Neither need you do anything but be yourself. LAO-TSE

A Shinto bride wears white to symbolize a new beginning; the typical white headpiece known as *tsunokakushi* symbolically hides her "horns of anger" at the prospect of her future husband's infidelity.

White represents purity, simplicity, and openness. Druids and ancient priests as well as clergy in the present-day Church of England wore white when they officiated at sacred services. Traditionally, white animals were sacrificed to appease gods in Roman, Persian, and European ceremonies.

Sometimes in order to go forward you have to go back to earlier times when the path you were just starting out on was still covered in virgin snow. This will help you work out whether you are on the right track for you. You may have some strong reactions as you uncover earlier memories but this is all part of thawing frozen creativity so you can reconnect to earlier spontaneity. Write your answers in your Creative Year Journal. Work quickly so you don't have time to censor yourself.

✳ My favorite childhood game was . . .
✳ The best TV program I ever saw as a child was . . .

* My earliest memory of school was . . .

* The toy I loved most was . . .

* If I had had a perfect childhood I would have grown up to be . . .

* The best gift anyone could have given me as a child would have been . . .

- Look back at your answers. What do they tell you about the way you started off? What hints do they give you about the start of your journey, which has taken you to where you are now?

Remember, it is always possible to retrace your steps and find another track that suits the person you are in your heart of hearts. Maybe the "road less traveled" is the one for you.

Green tendrils of growth

Green is the color of growth and of hope and is associated with fertility and fruition. It is a positive color to use when you are contemplating new ventures as it is made up of cool blue and hot yellow so it brings balance.

Sometimes it is useful to go back to basics, to find out what influences you and your well-being. Like plants, we all need good roots, support, and stimulation to fulfill our creative potential.

Roots: Do you need more contact with your family or to spread your roots further, to reach down into connections with people past or present, who can offer you creative or emotional nourishment? Make a list of people who you could contact.

Support: Maybe you could do with shelter from the elements in the form of a cozy base from which to explore as you become more exposed. You could invest in building up your physical strength too. Make a list of activities that could build up your stamina.

Stimulation: By being aware of your aim you can move toward it just as a plant grows toward the light. To blossom creatively you have to learn to trust the inner voice that says, "This feels good, this feels like it is what I was meant to do." Hear it and give yourself room to heed it, even though it may seem strange. The inner urge to completion is a vital part of the process of creativity; it is the intuitive that speaks through every gene of our body.

Red danger, red roses

The morning star is like a man; he is painted red all over; that is the color of life. TRADITIONAL PAWNEE CHANT

Red brings passion, danger, and strong emotions. It can give you a burst of energy when you are low. This exercise will help you to access the vibrational energy of red.

✳ Collect various red objects, such as a red apple, a red pepper, red onions, and some red flowers or red plants.

✳ Arrange them in front of you and just sit close to them. Be aware of any changes in your mood or feelings. Nothing may happen; it may be that you don't need more of this vibrational energy than you have right now. Just be open to possibilities. Note any feelings and ideas in your Creative Year Journal.

✳ Next get some red crayons or pencils and draw the shapes of the objects you chose. Color them in very thickly, using each hand in turn. Don't worry about going over the edges; free yourself from the constraints of boundaries. Feel your blood coursing through your hands and arms as you use the red.

✳ When you have finished sit back and absorb the different reds before you.

✳ In your Creative Year Journal note any feelings you have or thoughts about the influence of red at this point.

Blue bliss

Blue is the color of loyalty, devotion, and true love, so brides are entreated to wear "something old, something new, something borrowed, and something blue," for "marry in blue, your love will be true." Blue bead amulets are worn as a protection against illness and the "evil eye" in many Middle Eastern countries.

The negative side of blue is "the blues," those times when we feel low and dispirited. This activity will help you to shift those feelings into a positive place. Write down your responses in your Creative Year Journal under the title "Blue's Day Out."

* Imagine your "blue" feelings are a person called "Blue," who needs to go out to see a fresh vista and needs some tender loving care.

* Where would you walk with Blue? In the park, beside a river, up a valley?

* Where would you take Blue for a drink? And what drink? A latte in a café, a cocktail at a bar, a soda at the ice-cream parlor, or maybe fresh orange juice at the Ritz?

* What music would you play to lighten Blue's spirit? A samba, a little Chopin, or perhaps some folk music?

* What present would thrill your friend Blue? A clear crystal, a posy of spring flowers, or sugar cane to make life sweeter?

* Add some "quality time" ideas of your own.

Yellow brilliance

Yellow is the color of the sun, on which all life depends. Yellow is the color of Athena, the goddess of wisdom. Invoking her support will add to your sense of confidence. It is the color of intuition, bringing flashes of brilliance to inspire new ideas.

Yellow is also a transition color; it signals a time between stop and go. Yellow is called the toxic eliminator. If our skin and the whites of our eyes turn yellow it is because our liver is not functioning properly and we are not eliminating the toxic wastes. This can happen on a psychological level too. In this exercise you can explore the power of yellow to help you eliminate things that are no longer of any use to you.

* Imagine yourself bathed in yellow light—the rays of the sun, a stage spotlight with a yellow filter, or light shining though yellow silk.

* Think of worn-out ideas, habits, legacies, and beliefs that block you. Common ones include: "Nothing works out for me," "I'll never be a success," "No one will ever love me."

* Avoid "ever" and "never" words; they kill creativity and enhance negativity.

* In your Creative Year Journal make a list of those negative thoughts that swirl around your head when you can't get to sleep at night or that haunt you at three in the morning. When you have a complete list, turn them into positives. We'll come back to them in the last section, Creative Completion.

Shocking pink

Pink is the passion of red softened by white. In its positive light it is the color of the feminine, gentle and soft, which neutralizes aggression. It calms and quietens, but sometimes pink has a twist, which is what the famous fashion designer Schiaparelli found when she introduced "Shocking Pink." This is beyond the sweetness of cotton candy and is much more provocative.

It is much easier to stay inside your "comfort zone," to do those things that feel fine but that don't challenge you very much. Let's try to move beyond that, to step outside the box.

The following are some phrases that use the word pink. Try and think up some more of your own to help loosen your self-censorship.

"**Pink elephants**"—hallucinations brought on by drunkenness.

"**In the pink**"—in good health.

"**Pink-hi**"—Australian for holiday or celebration especially among Aborigines.

How else could you apply more shocking pink to your life? Why not throw a shocking pink party—no dull tones allowed—or award friends who make you laugh till it hurts a shocking pink certificate. Imagine a shocking pink passport that lets you go to shocking pink places.

Going for gold

Carl Jung wrote that 90 percent of the shadow is pure gold. From what appears to be a crisis, a terrible misadventure, or a dreadful diagnosis can come the most important learning of your life.

Shadows only appear because the sun shines. Without that brightness we could not have the dark contrast. If we think of shadows as sad or difficult emotions, stretches in our life that were intense or traumatic, we can also sieve through the pain to the gold learning that is there. For example, one of my clients had horrific nightmares following the death of her brother. As part of the therapeutic process I asked her to paint the images that came to her. Now, three years later, she attends art classes and exhibits her work; she has started to sell her work too. Something positive came from the "valley of the shadow of death." It's never too late to be what you've always wanted to be. Forget the "I might have been;" think, "I can still be more true to my hearts' desire."

• In your Creative Year Journal make a note of some of the shadows in your life and find a nugget of gold that came from each experience.

Black beauties

Darkness was at first by darkness hidden. HINDU CREATION MYTH

For desert people, black denotes life because black clouds bring the rain that allows the plants to grow. Black is linked to fertility since most seeds need darkness to germinate. In Europe and the United States, black is connected to funerals and mourning, night and evil. Yet it is also associated with good luck in the form of a black cat or a chimney sweep.

Delving the black depths without light can be frightening. It may evoke childhood fears of the dark, but in those depths you may find the greatest jewels to add to your creative collection. In the words of Theodore Roethke, "In a dark time, the eye begins to see." In this exercise the idea is to help you see the great beauty in black and to recognize the way light and dark work together to enhance the power of both.

* Imagine a black sky with white stars shining or think of a black velvet blanket scattered with diamonds.

* Get a piece of card the size of a postcard. Randomly cover it with colors using crayons. Use the color thickly and include white.

* Using black, cover the entire surface so that the first colors are hidden.

* With the point of a nib or a small knife, scrape away some of the black crayon to reveal the colors below. Make your own night sky studded with glowing stars.

Color credit cards

This is your personal color therapy kit, which you can use whenever you need an extra splash of vibrational energy to help you along. It is combined with affirmations—statements to reaffirm what already is, though you might not have recognized. This activity will boost both your confidence and your ability to attract abundance into your life.

✳ Assemble different colored cards each cut to a uniform size about the same size as a credit card. You will also need a pen and a list of affirmations. (You will find many in my book *Creative Visualization with Color* or you can write your own or look at those in the Creative Writing section.)

✳ Divide your cards into seven piles, one for each day of the week. On one side write the name of the day of the week and on the other side a color affirmation. For example: "I surround myself with the clarity of blue;" "Today I am filled with the wisdom of yellow;" "Orange brings me energy to unite others;" "The passion of red fuels my day;" and "The purity of white illuminates all my decisions today." There will be forty-nine cards, seven for each day of the week.

✳ Each day choose a card, look at the message, and place it in your wallet. You could also share them with a friend or family.

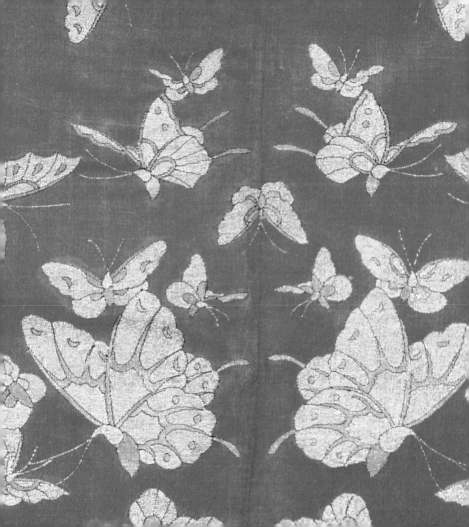

Month 8

Creative Abundance

Abundance is the sense of plenty, fullness, and benevolence. It can never come purely from material wealth; some of the richest people in the world have desperately unhappy lives because they feel a lack of love or of self-acceptance. True abundance comes from accepting who you are and believing that your place in the universe is meant to be and that the universe gives you what you need.

This chapter shows you how to tap into your vast reserves of creativity to excavate your personal source of emotional well-being and connect to the rest of our generous universe. You will collect objects and make diagrams to show how you invest your talents and energy and discover how you can expand these. In addition, you will create a coat of arms to attract plenty and make a frieze to celebrate the abundance of what the universe has already given you, which you may not yet have recognized.

Creative living is a way of seeing the world anew all the time. Every experience is fresh and is able to amaze us. When you feel surprised at yourself you are being creative, when you delight in small things you are being open to the vitality of life. Learning to trust your originality gives you the opportunity to become more and more creative and recognize the true abundance that surrounds you every moment of your life.

The eighth path

After passing through the seven stages or heavens, the spiritual seeker, the initiate, reaches her goal. Traditionally eight is the number of paradise rediscovered. It is connected with rebirth, resurrection, and renewal. In the Judeo-Christian tradition, God made the world in seven days and on the eighth, life began to be lived. In Buddhism the number eight represents completion. There are eight signs of good fortune and the Noble Eightfold Path teaches the way to *nirvana*: right knowledge, right attitude, right speech, right action, right livelihood, right effort, right state of mind, and right concentration.

Questionnaire

There is great pressure on us to conform to the pressures of "should." You "should" work hard to gain the good opinion of others, wear the right clothes to show your status, and pass examinations to gain respect. However, when caught up in an extreme situation we may find that those "shoulds" don't allow us to express what we really value.

Think about the following situations to discover what you really value.

* If your home was on fire and you could safely rescue one item, what would it be?

* If you could stop your usual work or routine for six months, what would you do?

* What would give your life more meaning right now?

✳ What "gift" would you give to a newly born child?

✳ If you knew you had five years to live, what would you do?

Feedback

• Did you choose something of financial value or something that held a special memory? If you rescued something that connects you to a loved person or special person, think about how your life reflects the value you attach there. Do you give time to nurture and cherish the relationship or the memory?

• Six months is long enough to do something you have always longed to do. Did you choose to rest? In that case, do you look after your physical and emotional health well enough? Perhaps you chose to do something completely different. In that case, what could you do now to make that dream a reality?

• Was your choice to do with spending more time with people you love, following a path of meditation and reflection, or achieving a goal? Do these reflect what you desire or are they choices others have said you should make?

• Your "gift"—beauty, kindness, love, and wealth—reflects what you would like more of in your life now.

• If you chose to continue to do what you are doing now, it sounds as if you value your life fully. If you chose a complete change, reflect on how you can live your life more fully now.

Today is the day we know we have, tomorrow is a hope. Live your values each and every day.

Collecting pebbles

A pebble, a small stone rounded by water that flows over it in the seas or rivers, is a simple object, yet it carries the wonder of our natural world.

Ursula Le Guin, the famed writer of the *Earthsea Trilogy,* collects pebbles. Throughout her house and garden are stones and rocks from all over the world. Wherever she travels she brings back a reminder, a small moment captured in the solidity and strength of a pebble.

The following true story demonstrates the power of simple abundance. A man was diagnosed with late-stage cancer; his prognosis was not very hopeful. His friends around the world phoned or wrote to him asking what they could do to help. The man didn't lack money or possessions but he recognized that his friends wanted to give him something as a symbol of their love. "Find a small pebble, one that touches your heart, and send that to me. I know that will touch my heart too." Pebbles came every day. Soon he had a wonderful collection of all shades and sizes, and each time he caressed their smooth surfaces he felt calmed and loved. For many years he appreciated the healing love of his friends, symbolized by the potent pebbles.

Start your own collection of pebbles. When choosing them, look for distinctive features that appeal to you, and in your Creative Year Journal record where and in what circumstances you found them.

Attracting abundance

In the ceaseless activity of the world we often lose touch with our creative selves, bombarded as we are by sounds, colors, neon signs, and blaring traffic. When we make time to stop, look, and listen we open our hearts to the gifts of the universe. Close your eyes for a moment and think about what true abundance or prosperity means to you. Breathe deeply and allow your thoughts and feelings to rise to the surface.

✳ Think about the work you have done in the past, paid or unpaid, voluntary or on your vacations. Make a list of those jobs. What patterns can you see? Are they people centered or is it the completion of tasks that feature most?

✳ Think about the friendships you have had. What attracted you to those people and what did they like about you? Can you see a pattern in those relationships? For example, are you the good listener who is there in times of need?

✳ Consider the patterns you have noted. What can you see in terms of energy? How much positive energy have you put into the jobs you loved and the people you love? The more positive energy you generate the more abundance you attract.

The educated heart

You cannot teach a man anything: you can help him to find it for himself. GALILEO GALILEI

How open are you to the wonders of the world? Do you let in new experiences or do you stay trapped in your own perceptions, believing and seeing what you've always believed or seen?

When Captain John Ross wrote *Voyage of Discovery* in 1819, he described how the "eskimeaux," or Inuit, who had never seen a European masted ship before, believed that the *Isabella* and *Alexander* were great birds. Understandably, it took some time to persuade them that they had nothing to fear from the ships. Sometimes we, too, cannot see or accept what is in front of our eyes. We need to retrain our vision to take account of the magical abundance that surrounds us.

In the following activity we explore the wonders that are part of everyday life but that we may close our eyes to. To connect to the ingenuity of what makes us human we will explore what has gone before. If we can learn to appreciate that more fully we can celebrate the wonder of our fellow human beings in our life today.

This activity takes half a day. Dress comfortably and take yourself off to a museum that has collections from earlier communities.

On the small island of Mull in Scotland there is a collection of old farming implements and domestic utensils that look as if they came out of the ark. In the Smithsonian in Washington there are exotic costumes and tools from all corners of the world. If there is no museum close to where you live, take a trip to the anthropological section of your local library or use a computer to surf the World Wide Web.

✳ Look at clothes, utensils, and objects. Notice the decorations, colors, and the skill in making these artifacts without the use of modern machinery. Open yourself to the wonder of what human beings are capable of, and that includes you.

✳ Make a note of what surprises and impresses you.

✳ Celebrate their creativity by making a copy of some of the decorations; think about how you express your creativity.

Personal wealth

What nature delivers to us is never stale, because what nature creates has eternity in it. ISAAC BASHEVIS SINGER

Personal finances take up a great deal of time: thinking about how to make enough to live on, how to make more, how to become wealthy, and then how to keep wealthy. Whichever part of the financial continuum you are on, it has its challenges. It also represents power and our attitude toward it tells us a lot about our view of abundance.

* Look at the following list. Write down which words correspond to your own idea of what money represents to you: security, power, opportunity, freedom, escape, oppression, corruption, materialism, fun, generosity, legacies, greed, success, abundance, status, evil.

* Add more definitions of your own.

Think about what you have chosen. Often our fears about wealth prevent us from achieving it because we feel it will change us for the worse, so we sabotage ourselves. The way we relate to wealth often reflects our attitudes to ourselves, as Shakti Gawain reveals in her book *Creating True Prosperity*. If you feel worthless you are hardly likely to let wealth come your way, financial or emotional. If you have a great deal of money and are afraid someone will cheat you, then you will be unlikely to enjoy the benefits it can offer.

Check out your attitude to personal wealth and recognize that it involves much more than money. If you thought you had to wait until you came into a fortune before you experienced abundance, by now you will have recognized that true abundance does not live in a bank vault.

Personal prosperity

How can we be prosperous when we are riddled with jealousy? We are taught to "beware the green-eyed monster," the envious one who pushes us to resent and hate others. Instead of repressing such feelings, however, embrace them—learn more about them. The following exercise can be uncomfortable, but you will gain greater insight if you explore your feelings of jealousy. By turning your feelings around you can heal the wound that jealousy reveals.

* Write the names of three people who bring out feelings of jealousy in you. Perhaps they got something you wanted: the job, the partner, the success, the looks, the perfect life?
* Write down why you are jealous.
* What have you got that this person has not or which they might value?

Sometimes jealousy alerts us to feelings of hunger of the soul, hunger that was not satisfied earlier and that prevents us from experiencing abundance. Gianni was jealous of the success of Satish, who was rich and could travel anywhere in the world because he had no commitments. When Gianni thought about what he had of value he recognized that he had two children and a partner he'd been with for eight years. He owned his feelings and understood that for him, his family was more sustaining than tourist resorts and unlimited air miles.

The frieze of fortune

This exercise gives you the chance to truly value the gifts life has given you and to celebrate your efforts in making good things happen. It involves some delving and excavating into your past success and may take time to gather the resources you need, but it will be worth every minute.

You will need: • A strip of paper or card about three feet long and ten inches wide. • Scissors and glue, pen or pencil.

✳ Think back over your life and note any high points. This exercise is for you; choose what felt good to you without considering what other people thought. Others have included the following choices: "When I was picked for the hockey team when I was eleven," "The time I played Juliet in *Romeo and Juliet*," "The day I met Richard," "The afternoon we had a picnic and I fell into the stream."

✳ Now collect any material you have that records these events. This could include photocopies of diary entries, photographs, newspaper clippings, letters or postcards, or theater or sports programs. If you don't have access to these perhaps you have friends or family who do. This is an opportunity to make contact and ask them. You don't need to keep the original. You can photocopy or scan it into a computer to get a printout.

✳ Arrange your material on the card to make a frieze, or sequence of events. Write about the events if you wish to or leave the images to speak for themselves. Your frieze of fortune reflects the many events that have made your life fortunate; find a place to display it so it will remind you of the abundance in your life.

The gift of gratitude

You pray in your distress and in your need, would that you might pray also in the fullness of your joy and in the days of your abundance.   KAHLIL GIBRAN

Gill Edwards, in her book *Living Magically,* describes her belief that our inner world and the way we think influences our outer world and the people we attract into our lives. They mirror our inner world.

The science of psychoneuroimmunology shows that the way we feel affects our nervous system, which in turn influences our immune system. When we feel good our immune system is strengthened, but when we feel low and negative it is weakened.

Good health is an important part of abundance. When we are ill we do not recognize that energy is the basic currency in the process of healing. In the following activity you will celebrate the positive energy your body gives and gain a boost for your immune system.

✳ Make a list in your Creative Year Journal of parts of your body and major organs. Now write a "thank you" to each part on the list. Here are some examples: "Thank you, heart, for beating nonstop through thick and thin"; "Thank you, legs, for holding me up when my world turned upside down."

✳ Read your list of thanks out loud.

My coat of arms

There is no wealth but life.   JOHN RUSKIN

A coat of arms was originally worn over a knight's armor so that the heralds, the men who announced the tournaments, could tell one knight from another. The coat of arms carried symbols and images that distinguished each wearer and told of his family, strengths, and position.

In this exercise you are going to design your own coat of arms in the shape of a shield. The shield both protects the owner and announces her attributes; by focusing on your strengths you attract more abundance into your life.

✳ Draw the shape of a shield on a piece of card big enough to cover your chest.

✳ Divide it into four sections by making a cross from top to bottom and right to left.

✳ In each section draw one of the four images described below—ancestors, creature, personal symbol, and motto—that tells your story.

Ancestors: What is the story of your family? What can represent it? Perhaps three wavy blue lines to show you are descended from immigrants? A log cabin to represent early pioneers? Think about the strengths that ensured the survival of your family and find a simple way to depict them.

Creature: Many coats of arms included real or imaginary creatures, which represented the strengths the person wanted to have. A phoenix demonstrated the ability to rise from the ashes, to overcome adversity. A lamb represented purity, whereas a bull symbolized power and resolve. Choose a creature to represent the qualities that empower you.

Personal symbol: What do you wish to be recognized for? Think about what makes you uniquely you. This can be difficult and it helps if you think about what your closest friends value in your relationship. Your kindness or peace-making qualities? Your humor and ability to rise above obstacles? Think about an image that captures you and use that as your personal symbol. Some symbols chosen by others include a dove, a rose, an artist's palette, a feather, and a set of scales.

Your motto: Is there a family saying you could put here or a quotation that holds significance for you? Is there an affirmation that helps when times are tough? You might find a book of quotations helpful, so give yourself time to choose something truly inspirational.

• Remember to think about the power of color and to choose those that represent you.

Planet of plenty

The paintings of the surrealist Remedios Varo (1908–1963) delight the eye and heart with fine details and strange, dreamlike images. Like fellow surrealist Leonora Carrington, she spoke of the need for a reconciliation with nature. For both painters there were no barriers between the ordinary, the everyday, and the magical. As Marina Warner said in her introduction to Carrington's *The Seventh Horse and Other Stories,* "There are no hierarchical differences between the cooking pot and the alchemist's alembic, between the knitting of a jumper and the weaving of the soul from 'cosmic wool.'" In other words, however mundane we think our life is, it has a magical quality. Every act is miraculous.

To really appreciate the abundance of our planet we need to stop and pay attention. When we do this we realize just how rich our lives are.

✳ Find a quiet place in your home. Look at whatever is around you. Choose three objects and think about what went into making them. Who made them? Where did they come from and what original materials were used in their production? For example, if you have a pencil that is made of wood and graphite, it was probably made in a factory somewhere. Originally the wood was a growing tree and the graphite, a form of carbon, was formed in the earth. Your connection to this planet of plenty is in everything you touch.

✳ Trace the lines of connection back to the earth and consider what you can do to sustain the planet that nurtures you.

The blessing of balance

Just a little more loving and a lot less fighting and the world would be all right. MAE WEST

Keeping a balance emotionally is every bit as important as keeping a healthy bank balance. Going too far into debt, giving away too much of yourself in caring for others, can lead to emotional bankruptcy, also known as burnout. When you reach that stage you cannot care for anyone, let alone yourself.

* Draw a set of scales in your Creative Year Journal. On one side put a plus sign and on the other a minus sign.

* On the plus side write down all the things that make you feel good, light, and happy, and that bring you joy.

* On the minus side write down all the parts of your life that make you sad, unhappy, or stressed.

* Imagine that each word weighs two pounds. Add up the words on each side and convert their number to pounds. Is it weighted on one side? What do you need to achieve a balance? Think about what you can discard or include to improve the balance in your life.

賜進士出身翰林院檢討江蘇徐海道　賞戴藍翎

敕授文林郎壬子科舉人江蘇試用縣知縣前任翁源

賜進士出身翰林院編修江南道監察御史協理京畿道事務誥授奉直大

賜進士出身翰林院庶吉士宗愚姪　　衍桐

以予言為河漢也予故悉著之以為異日之左驗

辛酉科舉人姻家晚生楊俊邦　　己酉科舉人宗愚弟　斯港

丁卯科恩副貢姻家晚生藍作藩　　丁卯科武舉愚又姻孫壻張德斌

姻家侍教弟國學李昭明　　愚內弟鄉飲程培和

愚壻侯選同知藍重潤　　愚姪壻貢生繆經獻

愚姪孫壻邑庠蘇樾謨　國學游啟欽　朱希程

宗姪恩貢　霖　邑廩鴻鈞　邑廩家祥　邑

愚姪職員德光　　職員超鰲　　國學仰麟　職員友竹　處

貢生應權　邑庠名瑞　廩生心文　邑庠裕光　國

鄉賓光泰　貢生星淮　貢生寶忠　國學惠國　邑

邑庠文江　邑庠文藻　邑庠壽祺　武庠步廷　國

附貢斌　國學和　　邑廩　　郎庠瀾　郎庠芬　邑

同治十年歲

Month 9

Creative Writing

In Old English, *writan*, the word from which writing derives, meant to scratch runes into bark. A rune is a character derived from the Roman alphabet and each was believed to have magical significance. Words still have this magical power; when we write we share knowledge and may influence others and the course of history. We can make words magical so that they become our personal runes.

All writing is a creative act. This month we will explore many techniques to free the inner muse so that your creative spirit can emerge. We will make lists, create poems, collect quotes, write letters we might never post, and meet the wordsmith who dwells within.

When we write, we anchor our thoughts and ideas. We give expression to our inner world and make feelings manifest. In writing you can bear witness to past hurts and triumphs. Writing is an act of reclamation, getting back what we have lost or may never have spoken of.

These writing exercises give you the opportunity to clarify your thoughts and feelings and to create wonderful stories that you can share with others if you so choose. Whether you write for yourself, your friends or children, or for the public, writing will give your creative self a voice.

The ninth path

The ancient Greeks called nine a mystical number because it consists of three lots of three, the trinity of trinities. This theme was taken up by John Milton in *Paradise Lost* when he described nine muses, nine earths, and nine rivers of hell. The Irish god Donn, Lord of the Dead, is the mythical ancestor god who lives in a cave and is surrounded by nine maidens who fan the fire of the magic cauldron. There are nine serpents of Nagas that are worshiped in southern India.

Other nines in popular use include "dressed to the nines," looking perfect from head to toe; "a nine days' wonder," something that causes a great stir when it first happens but is soon forgotten; and "cloud nine," a heavenly place to be where you feel wonderful.

The ninth month of the year is of great significance to Muslims, who mark Ramadan by fasting during daylight hours. It is believed that Mohammed received the words of Allah during Ramadan and so this time must be kept holy. It ends with the joyous festival of Eid ul-fitr.

Questionnaire

✳ Where do you write most? At work, at home, in a writing group, on holiday?

✳ What type of writing do you do—business plans, progress reports, postcards from holiday locations, letters or e-mails to friends?

✳ As a child, what stories did you like to read and write?

✳ Is there a form of writing that you prefer to read now?

✳ If you could choose to write anything at all what would it be?

Feedback

• Where you write usually dictates the type of writing you do. Work in an insurance company, for example, will usually demand factual writing that is very specific, whereas writing in an advertising agency may be much freer.

• Think about what pleasure you get and the skills you use in the writing you do. The skills in one area can transfer to more creative writing. For instance, writing a list of objectives at work is similar to making a list of aims for a piece of fiction.

• Fairy tales, tales of adventure, and mysteries are firm favorites with children. What you enjoyed in childhood forms the basis for your taste today. If you were put off writing and reading in school, now is the time to reconnect to the joy of writing.

• Your choice of reading now will help you to choose the form of writing you would like to try. If you enjoy reading romantic fiction you are unlikely to get a great deal of pleasure writing a Gothic horror novel filled with fear and gore, so start with what you enjoy.

• Whatever you choose to write, give it a title. For example, if you choose poetry think of a title for a poem and write it down. Don't worry what comes next, just let a title come into your mind and record it in your Creative Year Journal. When you finish the activities in this section, go back to that title and see if you can use some of the writing you've produced to develop your piece.

Spontaneous writing

Spontaneous or "stream of consciousness" writing has been favored by writers such as James Joyce, Virginia Woolf, and Jack Kerouac. It involves putting pen to paper and writing whatever comes into your head without stopping or judging, censoring or evaluating. It enables you to get over blocks such as "What will I write?" and "Will it be good enough?"

Virginia Woolf explained that the process worked for her because it gave her no time to hesitate; she included everything and in the process found "the diamonds of the dust heap."

* Set an alarm clock for seven minutes.

* Set down the title, "Things I Have Seen," and begin to write.

* When the alarm goes, stop writing. Then set it again for a further seven minutes.

* Begin writing about "Things I Have Not Seen."

* Stop as soon as the alarm goes off.

* Now, read what you have written and underline any words or phrases you find striking.

* You can now go on to develop what you have written further or you can use the underlined words as the basis for an entirely different piece, maybe a poem or a short story. Use this type of writing as a limbering-up exercise to prepare your mind and body for in-depth writing.

Your muse

Why does my muse only speak when she is unhappy?
She does not, I only listen when I am unhappy.
When I am happy I live and despise writing
For my Muse this cannot but be dispiriting.
STEVIE SMITH, "MY MUSE," 1964

The nine daughters of Zeus and Mnemosyne were goddesses of different arts and sciences and from them we get the word muse, which means a goddess who inspires us to create. As the poet Stevie Smith says above, often we do not listen to our muse unless we are unhappy. However, if you want to invite your muse to visit you can do so now. The following exercise is a way of playfully getting a picture of your muse.

Complete these prompts and be as inventive and free as you can as you imagine your muse:

∗ If my muse were a bird she would be ...

∗ If my muse were a color she would be ...

∗ If my muse were an animal she would be ...

∗ If my muse were a sound she would be ...

∗ If my muse were a taste she would be ...

∗ If my muse were a tree she would be ...

✳ If my muse were a texture she would be . . .

✳ If my muse were a part of the landscape she would be . . .

Now write them out again, beginning each line with "I am" and then adding your choices, perhaps with an additional description. Here is an example:

MY MUSE

I am a soaring eagle.
I am indigo in a dark sky.
I am a solitary polar bear.
I am Tibetan bells.
I am fresh mangoes.
I am a mighty oak.
I am soft velvet.
I am the snow capped tops of the Himalayas.
I am part of you.

The last line, "I am part of you," completes your poem.

Life lists

Japanese ladies of the court in medieval China wrote journals, known as pillow books. Sei Shonegan, born circa 965, was partial to including lists in her pillow book; for example, under "things that should be short" Sei Shonegan listed:

A piece of thread when one wants to sew something in a hurry.

A lamp stand.

The speech of a young girl.

What would your list of "things that should be short" be like? Perhaps it would include a visit to the dentist; a cool period between friends; the time between hunger and eating; or the length of a recovery?

Lists can be about anything. They play a central role in the best-selling book *Bridget Jones's Diary*, where the heroine lists the food she has eaten, the number of cigarettes she has smoked, and the units of alcohol consumed, all in a desperate attempt to control her life and find Mr. Right. Rob, the central character in Nick Hornby's *High Fidelity*, uses lists to maximum effect as a means of sorting out his life and relationships.

✳ Choose one of the following titles: "Journeys I've Made," "Music I've Heard," or "Places I've Been."

✳ Write down twelve items under your chosen heading.

Here's an example for "Cities I've Visited":

• Manchester • New York • Paris • Tehran • Santa Fe • London • Rome
• Melbourne • Santa Cruz • Dublin • Edinburgh • Granada • San Francisco

Next to each city put a word or phrase to describe your feelings about the place and its impact on you.

Manchester—lights reflecting on rainy streets.

New York—subways and Mario's pizzas.

Paris—Easter sunshine on the Seine.

Tehran—the call from the mosque through still air.

Next add human interest, maybe someone you met there or someone who looked amazing. Add that to your list. Soon you'll find you have the bones of a poem or a story, or even sections for your autobiography.

Keeping a journal

Words can enlarge us and they can shrivel us. The words we use contain our breath, the breath of life. We make our world out of our language and the stories we tell shape our world. Many people feel compelled to write because the voice that resides within will not be still or quiet. In keeping a journal—writing down whatever we feel like, whenever we can—we do not have the tyranny of a diary that must be completed every day.

You already have many entries in your Creative Year Journal. Now might be a good time to look through and see what themes are emerging and to consider if there are any areas you would like to develop.

Journals help us to make sense of the world. As we try to put the events of our life on paper they becomes less overwhelming; in the process we work out ideas and feelings that have been fermenting and foaming in our mind. Writing reorders our experience and lets us release emotions in a safe way.

Travel gives an ideal opportunity to write. V. S. Naipaul describes his travel writing as the "writing of inquiry," which is as much to do with the inner journey as the outer world we pass through.

This exercise will help you develop your journal writing technique.

Choose the place you are in now or go to a place where you feel comfortable and that is a place familiar to you. You will write down everything you feel, hear, taste, touch, and smell. The idea is to capture the moment and to include every little detail, thereby expanding your ability to observe.

* Write down what you can see in detail, including color, patterns, textures, and changes that happen.

* Write down everything you can hear, including snatches of mechanical sound, conversation, and the sound of your pen on paper.

* Write down the tastes that surround you, the bitter taste of stale coffee, the acidity of a lemon, or the sweetness of honeysuckle.

* Describe the sense of touch as, in your mind's eye, you reach and stroke, prod, and caress what is around you.

* All the smells that you encounter have a place on your page, so include them too.

When you write in this way you capture the heart of your experience on every level that strikes your senses. If you do this regularly you build up excellent observation skills and clarity of writing.

Writing rituals

The pages are still blank, but there is a miraculous feeling of the words being there, written in invisible ink and clamoring to become visible. VLADIMIR NABOKOV

There are many writing rituals that might help you to keep going when the creative process slows down. Here are some used by well-known writers:

• Philip Pullman, author of *His Dark Materials Trilogy*, approaches each new book like an engineer with pieces of narrative and ideas stuck on a storyboard to be developed, moved, or altered. He is open to the way the story develops and is often taken by surprise.

• Roald Dahl wrote in his garden shed. He had a wooden board on which he rested his writing paper and wrote longhand. He would never allow anyone to clean the shed or disturb him there.

• Jonathan Gash is a professor of medicine as well as a novelist. He writes on scraps of paper between appointments, in taxis, when he is waiting for his wife, in fact at any odd moment he has. He goes home and sticks the scraps on a corkboard that lines three walls of his office. He moves the papers about as he sees links between the writing and so a story emerges.

Other writers begin at a certain time and have a set number of words they must write before they allow themselves to finish. Some make sure that they have written the sentence that will begin the next writing day.

You will discover your own writing rituals. Whatever they are, the essential part is to allow yourself some definite time once a week or preferably once a day to write. Fit it around your life as it is and give yourself permission to be creative. Remember, you can work on your written words but you cannot worry them into existence. Make a list of writing rituals that would suit the life you lead.

The legacy others have left us

The legacy of other people is part of the fabric of our lives. Strands of memories weave in and out of gifts we have been given or characteristics we have inherited. The legacy may be from family, friends, teachers, or others who influenced our lives. You can use all your memories to create wonderful writing, whether it is pure biography or the basis for a piece of fiction.

✳ This first exercise is a warm-up to get you thinking and to stir your memory. Look at your face in a mirror. In your Creative Year Journal, describe it in detail for as long as you can. Write about the memories you have of your face, what you looked like when you were younger, describe the wrinkles and the smile lines. As you look at your face think about who in your family has similar features to you. If you were adopted or never knew your biological parent(s), what do you imagine you share with them?

* All families have stories. Some are secret and forbidden, others are the source of history and may be lost if not recorded. Think about the stories you have heard about from your family, parents, grandparents, and extended family. Start a collection of these in your journal. Once you have basic details, extend them by finding out more information from the people whose stories they are, if that is possible, or research them by looking at contemporary newspapers in libraries or on the Internet.

* If you are anxious about setting down your family history in a factual and recognizable manner, you can set it out as fiction. Change characters, names, and identifying characteristics, dramatize events, and give different endings. This type of writing is very liberating as it allows you to lay to rest the ghosts that have haunted you.

Passionate poetry

up from the valley,
gold larch needles edge the lane;
stitching back my heart   GILLIE BOLTON

Creative writing has a therapeutic dimension, which is why it plays a prominent part in healthy living initiatives in Britain and the United States. Poetry has the power to heal both in the acts of reading it and of writing it. Research carried out by Dr. Robin Philipp from the University of Bristol has shown how poetry can be used in the treatment of anxiety, depression, and post-traumatic stress. Good poetry goes beyond time and place and has a universality that touches us all.

Part of the creative process is the letting go of daily thoughts in order to give space for creativity to blossom. American poet Robert Frost described how one evening he stepped out from his front door into the snowy darkness and the whole of his poem "Stopping by Woods on a Snowy Evening" came to him.

The woods are lovely, dark and deep.
But I have promises to keep,
And miles to go before I sleep,
And miles to go before I sleep.

✳ Think about the promises you have made to yourself, the promises you have to keep. Write them out, then set them down as a poem. They do not have to rhyme, though they might.

✳ Choose something that you feel passionately about and write down all the emotions you connect with it. Think about where you were when you felt these strong feelings first and describe that setting. If a person is involved, use short sentences to describe him or her. Use metaphors such as "She was a cat on the prowl" or "He was a vulture picking over the pieces." Now put them together, using repetition to strengthen the message.

It's not all straight lines

As spinners drew out their threads they told stories to pass the time and so "to spin a yarn" is to tell an imaginative tale. What raw material, like the fleece of a sheep, do you have to turn into a smooth crafted tale?

Stories, whether by the Brothers Grimm or Raymond Carver, allow us to travel into other lives and times. They also show us how to make sense of our own lives. When we tell our own story we realize it isn't all straight lines. There aren't fixed points that lead directly from A to B; rather, as the poet Philip Larkin put it, "a beginning, a muddle, and an end."

In the following exercise you use your words to make a pattern on the page so the visual aspect echoes the story. It adds interest and fun to your writing.

* Imagine you are a character from a fairy tale, for example, Little Red Riding Hood. Rewrite the story in her voice in short, simple sentences. As you write, change direction on the page every few sentences, so that the pattern of the words add to the story.

* Now put a dot in the middle of a fresh page of your journal. That is your starting point for a circular piece of writing. Your first words are "I thought I was going round in circles when . . ." Write about whatever comes to mind—a difficult time in a relationship, a journey when you were lost, or trying to explain a situation to someone who was on a completely different wavelength. As you write let your words go around and around so the pattern of the words mirrors the content.

Letters you never sent

How many times have you written a letter in your head but never got around to writing it? Many of us have longed to write and tell another person exactly what we thought and felt, yet feared the consequences.

Sometimes, separation or death intervenes and we lose the opportunity. However, it is never too late to write a letter that expresses your heartfelt feelings. You don't need to send it, you can burn it, throw it away, bury it, or place it in a special box for all those letters that you write and don't send. The process of writing the letter releases repressed emotions and frees you to move on in your life.

✳ Think of a person you wanted to communicate with and consider your greeting: Dear, My dearest, Hi.

✳ What do you want to say? Don't dress it up, speak from the heart.

✳ Add your thoughts, hopes, and disappointments and say why you found it hard to write this letter before. Pour out your feelings.

✳ How do you want to end your letter? Formally, "Yours sincerely," or from the heart, "With deepest love"? "In tears because you are no longer here" or "Thanks for being part of my life"?

✳ Now, decide what you want to do with your letter.

Affirmations

An affirmation is a positive statement. It usually begins with "I am" and is in the present tense. An affirmation is there to help you be "firm" about positive things about yourself and your life.

The more you repeat your affirmations the stronger the positive feelings become. You can use them anywhere at any time; you can say them to yourself or out loud. One of the best known affirmations is Emile Coué's "Every day, in every way, I'm getting better and better." Affirmations repeated in front of a mirror as you look into your own eyes are particularly empowering. Here are some examples of affirmations:

I am the master of my fate;
I am the captain of my soul.   WILLIAM ERNEST HENLEY

I am healthy, whole and complete.   LOUISE HAY

My heart is open to the grace of love.   BRENDA MALLON

• Choose areas of your life in which you want more positive action. Write some affirmations beginning with "I am."

• Write some of your affirmations on cards and place them in parts of your home where you will see them. These act as prompts to repeat the affirmations, which helps build up positive attitudes, which in turn influences the way you live your life.

CELEBRATION

As we approach the end of our creative journey, we prepare to rest and to renew our energies. In Creative Dreaming, Creative Spirituality, and Creative Completion we contemplate how far we have come along our creative journey, the challenges that we have faced, and how much we have managed to achieve over the last months. Now is the time for celebrating our efforts, rejoicing in our new talents, and looking forward to another year of renewal and growth.

Month 10

Creative Dreaming

Each night, as we sleep, we enter the dream world and spend, on average, two hours in a territory where our waking laws do not operate. We fly, travel great distances, meet strange animals and guides, and uncover our greatest potential. Dream adventures are not always pleasant; some take us to nightmarish borderlands where danger lurks. However, dreams bring us health and wholeness; dreams are our unique guidance system. This chapter shows how you can harness the power of your dream world.

There is deep yearning to understand what our dreams mean. In 2000 B.C.E. Artemidorus wrote a five-volume set on dream interpretation. This early record shows how the images in dreams reflected the worries, hopes, and desires of the early Greeks, just as our dreams today reflect our inner concerns. In working with our dreams we continue this ancient tradition that links the intuitive with the divine, the physical with the spiritual, and the present with the past and future.

Dreams make amazing connections that are often unavailable to the waking mind; they reveal the intuitive self working at a very deep level. When we appreciate the vast reservoirs of spontaneous, original connections that lie in our dreaming minds, then we find our dreaming self rewards us with yet more creative dreams.

The tenth path

The Hindu god Vishnu is responsible for controlling human fate. He appears in ten incarnations, or *avatars*. The two most important of these are Krishna and Rama. Guru Nanak (1469–1539 C.E.) was the founder of Sikhism and the first of ten gurus or teachers of the faith. There have to be ten men present for a full Jewish Orthodox service to take place; this is known as a *minyan*. The Ten Commandments given to Moses are the foundation of Judeo-Christian faith and summarize man's obligations to God. The followers of the Greek philosopher Pythagoras worshiped both four and ten because they were regarded as perfect numbers.

Questionnaire

* How do you feel about your dreams?

* What did you dream last night or what was the most recent dream you recall?

* What themes do you usually dream about?

* In your dreams are you usually passive, aggressive, or assertive?

* Do you have recurring dreams?

* Have you ever had a dream that changed your life?

Feedback

• How you feel about your dreams influences how you value them. The more you pay attention to them and respond to the information they offer, the more you gain.

• Recent dreams reflect current events or concerns in your life. They show you what matters below the surface and may offer solutions to present difficulties.

• There are universal dream themes such as falling, being chased, losing teeth, being lost or trapped, and flying, and others that include houses or cars. If there is one theme that predominates, it may well show you what it is you need to focus on in your waking life.

• How you behave in dreams indicates underlying traits. For example, if you are usually the "victim," being hurt or dismissed in some way, it may reflect how you act when awake.

• Recurring dreams will keep coming back until you respond to the message of the dream. Often they are about unfinished business that you may be denying when awake or they indicate aspects of your life you need to deal with. Recurring dreams indicate a need to do some waking work; when you do this the dreams change or disappear.

• "Numinous" or "big" dreams are those dreams you never forget. They have a powerful impact because of the intensity of feeling or imagery. If you have had such a dream think about how it influenced you and ask yourself if it has relevance to your life now.

Dream journal techniques

An uninterpreted dream is like an unopened letter.　　THE TALMUD

Recording your dreams is an important step in learning to interpret them.

* Keep a notebook by your bed. This will be your Dream Journal.

* Every morning, give yourself a few minutes to focus on your dreams. Let the images from your dreams form a bridge between your sleeping and waking life— the two are linked even though most of the time we don't appreciate the fact.

* Write down your dreams, unedited. Include it all because each has its place in revealing the meaning.

* Give your dream a title—this will help you remember it later.

* Draw dream images that are hard to describe with words.

* When you have time, return to the dream and consider how it relates to your life right now. Was there an event that triggered the dream, something that you might have experienced or witnessed that caused it? Think about any other connections and record them in your Dream Journal.

Images may be familiar or strange. Whatever the vision in your dream it is important to accept that it has some meaning for you. Ask yourself, "Why did I choose this image in my dream?" "What importance does this figure or shape or color hold for me?" Allow memories or associations to emerge in your answer. There usually is a link if you let yourself find it. Record these connections in your Dream Journal.

Dream incubation

William Blake, the English visionary and artist, wanted to make the most luminous illustrations possible for his poems and visions. One night he dreamed that his dead brother came and demonstrated a specific engraving technique that gave the shimmering color he so desired. It took conservationists over one hundred years to work out the technique he used. Blake called on his dreams to inspire him in many ways and we can ask for similar guidance today.

* Think about a problem you are concerned about at the moment. This can relate to work, to your health, to relationships, or to any other area of your life.

* On a piece of card write a request for a dream to help you solve the problem. For example, "Send me a dream to help me understand how I can get promotion" or "Let me have a dream that gives me guidance on the best way to recover from my illness."

* Place the card under your pillow. Write the request in your Dream Journal as well so that when you wake you can record your dream.

* Before you go to sleep, repeat the request. This will encourage your sleeping mind to work on the problem as you sleep.

✳ Once you have recorded your dream, work out what the message is. Remember that dreams work in symbols and metaphors, so look out for symbolic connections to your waking life.

✳ Be patient. It may take time to get the insight you desire.

Meeting your shadow

One does not become enlightened by imagining figures of light, but by making the darkness conscious.   CARL JUNG

The shadow is always with us, sometimes visible in the stark glare of midday but more often out of sight. It is the dark aspect of ourselves, what Jung called an archetype. Archetypes are inherited images that come from the deepest part of our unconscious and are shared by all people.

In all societies people dream of figures, animal or human, that in some way threaten the dreamer. They may be faceless and alien or have a sense of mysterious familiarity. Whatever the imagery associated with the shadow in your dreams, it represents an unrecognized aspect of yourself, part of that duality we looked at earlier. When we face the frightening shadowy being we can begin to accept ourselves completely. I'm reminded of the story "Peter Pan," who so longed for a shadow to make him human that he asked Wendy to make one and sew it on for him. Without our shadow we lack humanity.

In the dark you can see whatever is inside yourself and in dreams we explore this darkness. Just as we welcome silence when we want to listen to the inner, intuitive voice, so we can meet our hidden selves when we go through the door of dreams.

* Think back to negative elements in your dreams. Do they represent unhappy parts of your life now or in the past? Do they highlight problems you avoid?

* If you want to change the dream, imagine you are the scriptwriter of your dream—which you are—and then rewrite the script. What do you need to introduce to help you? How could you change the ending? By instigating the changes you are making it clear to yourself that you do have the power to transform your life, and this in turn alters your dreams.

Dreams that scare and teach us to dare

Fearful dreams and nightmares let us know that there are important issues we may be avoiding during waking life. Nightmares are wake-up calls that frequently show us that what we dismiss as trivial is in fact highly significant. They may also show how much a waking event has disturbed us. If we listen to their wisdom we find they bring new insights and fresh ways of seeing the world.

Carla had recurring dreams. In them, someone, usually a man, was trying to kill her and she had to fight for her life. At first she tried to ignore these nightmarish scenes but their insistence bothered her. She remembered reading that all dreams carry a message for the dreamer and decided to delve into her frightening dreamscapes.

She wondered why there were two people trying to suffocate her, because that, she realized, was how they were trying to kill her. Intuitively, she understood they were people she knew, though she couldn't explain why. "The dreams made me realize," she said, "that the two people suffocating me are my husband and myself." Though this revelation was a shock, she understood its truth. Her husband's excessive possessiveness and her own "acceptance" of his phobic jealousy were "suffocating" her.

* Think back to a frightening dream you have had.

* Imagine you are interviewing the person or thing that frightened you. You are awake and safe. Ask some questions: "What did you want?" "Why did you bother/hurt me?" Note your replies.

* Next, state out loud what you want this person/thing to do: "I want you to leave me alone." "Get out of my life." "Find a better place for yourself where you don't upset me."

Back to the future: childhood dreams

Some childhood dreams shape our whole lives. Carl Jung and Albert Einstein, as children, both had dreams that led them to devote their lives to understanding their meaning. Jung devoted his life to understanding the unconscious and Einstein wanted to know how light curved as it did in his dream.

✳ Close your eyes and think about the dreams you had as a child.

✳ When you recall a dream, record it in your Dream Journal, then give it a title.

✳ If you have difficulty, it may help to know some of the universal themes I found in my research for *Dream Time with Children*: flying, being chased, animals, being trapped, being lost, magical creatures.

✳ Can you relate your childhood dream to the path your life has taken? Does it give you guidance about what is most important to you?

Lucid dreams and taking control

In lucid dreams the dreamer is aware of dreaming and can influence what happens. Researchers such as Stephen La Berge at Stanford University, United States, and Keith Herne in Britain have found that lucid dreaming can be learned. With patience, care, and persistence you can learn to control your dreams, direct the action, decide what happens, and go wherever you want to travel.

The ability to control dreams often begins in childhood. Some children have a brief snatch of lucidity in disturbing dreams where, still in the dream, they say to themselves, "It's only a dream, I can wake up," and they do wake themselves up.

Lucid dreaming is a central part of the lives of "shamans," medicine men and women or "travelers between worlds." In their dreams they visit the realms of the spirits to learn healing power or gain knowledge that will help them or their community.

Characteristics of lucid dreaming

- Flying dreams are often the first indication of lucid dreaming.

- False awakenings. These follow the lucid dream and the person feels she has woken up, got ready for work, and so forth. Then some small detail that is out of place reveals that she is still dreaming.

- Lucid dream test. In your dream, test for gravity and pain. If you can fly you are dreaming; if you can feel pain you are probably awake.

- On waking, lucid dreamers may see dream images as if they are in their actual waking space. These are known as "hypnopompic hallucinations." They happen when the brain cannot switch smoothly from the dream to the waking state.

✳ Consider your dreams, from vivid childhood ones to those in more recent times. Have you had flying dreams? What are the most vivid images in your dreams?

* Once you have a strong image of a particularly vivid dream, maybe a room that recurs or a dream animal, try to fix the idea in your mind so that you will become conscious when you next come to this place in your dream. This imprinting can act as a trigger for lucid dreaming.

* Keep a record of these dreams.

Dreams that give birth to change

Dreams provide images that spark the creative galaxy within. Whether this is expressed in writing, drawing, painting, dance, music, or drama, the potential material from dreams is limitless.

The initiation into a new way of thinking, or onto a new path in life, is often heralded in a dream. These initiation dreams are to do with a start, a beginning, where a journey commences or an opening appears. They tell us that we are leaving behind that which has served its purpose so that we can embrace the new.

These dreams can include the following themes:

- Traveling in unknown territory.

- Crossing mountains or deserted plains.

- Passing over a narrow bridge or through a deep valley.

- Going through a maze or labyrinth.

- Elemental images of fire, water, air, and earth.

- A symbolic test or task the dreamer must accomplish.

- Symbolic rites such as baptism or death and rebirth.

Look through your dream records for any of these themes and be on the alert for them in future dreams.

The artist within

When we dream, the normal constraints of logical thinking are put on "standby," a bit like a computer that is on but not in use. Our system is still running but it is not taken up with the usual tasks. In human terms those are our daily activities. When we dream our mind transcends the mundane; our perception tunes into mind, body, and spirit and makes connections previously unavailable to us.

Dreams allow your conscious mind to work more creatively by linking ideas or words in ways that you would never have thought of when you were awake. These connections fascinated surrealists such as Dali, Magritte, and Goya, who tried to emulate the dream state in their paintings and sculptures.

Many writers and artists use dreams to inspire their creative life. Charlotte Brontë taught herself to dream about subjects she could not experience in waking life. Over a long period these "induced dreams" gave rise to what she called "a remarkable increase in creative inspiration." Robert Louis Stevenson dreamed of the plot of Dr. Jekyll and Mr. Hyde. His wife, Fanny, woke him as he screamed from his nightmare. He was furious because she had woken him from "a fine bogey tale." The dawn light found him frantically writing to capture the dream tale that is now known to millions.

The next time you have a dream, try making an image of it. Put the unusual combinations together and let yourself really play with the symbols. As you do this you are honoring your dream and celebrating your intuitive creativity. This inspires further creativity in your dream life.

Divine connections

The dream is a hidden door to the innermost recesses of the soul.
CARL JUNG

There is a large measure of agreement between communities worldwide, as there has been throughout history, that communication between this world and the next, between gods and mortals, between those still alive and others long dead, is possible in dreams. Many prophets and religious leaders have said they received divine instruction in their dreams. This might be in the form of angels, guides, or God himself. The Prophet Mohammed had his first revelation in a dream and received spiritual instruction that was profoundly important to the foundation of Islam.

In 2000 B.C.E. the Egyptian papyrus of Deral-Madineh gave examples of divine revelation and oracular dreams were consulted when decisions were made about matters of state. Egyptians even tried to communicate via dreams, perhaps an early recognition of telepathy, for they believed homeless spirits carried the message from one dreamer to another.

There is a widespread belief that the soul separates from the body when we dream. In dreams we enter a spiritual realm where the physical falls away, where we can meet friends and family who have died, where we can fly or find ourselves transported to different places or different worlds. From this position that the "conscious self" separates from the physical self when dreaming, it is not too far a leap to conclude that the "soul" that leaves the body in sleep can survive the death of the physical body.

✳ Think about any dreams that you have had in which you had a sensation of being out of your body or flying on a different plane.

✳ Consult your dream records to see if you have met any guides or divine presences. Guides may offer advice, reassurance, or healing. Such dreams leave the dreamer with a deep sense of peace and blessing.

Healing dreams

Dreams are important in maintaining emotional, physical, and spiritual well-being. Since early times they have been used in the diagnosis and treatment of illness. In Ancient Greece there were more than two hundred dream temples in which dream interpreters worked as doctors do today. Their patients came to dream and their dreams were used to discover the roots of the illness and the remedies that should be used.

You can use your dreams to enhance your health. Nourish your dreams and your dreams will nourish you.

* Think about any dreams in which parts of your body have been emphasized. Do you have any waking concerns about this part? If so, get a checkup.

* If you have dreamed about someone you know becoming ill it may indicate that you have noticed changes in their appearance or behavior that you have not consciously been aware of. This subliminal knowledge can apply to yourself as well, so think about what your dream could be telling you.

* If you have had dreams of monks it may signify healing, as hospital care was first offered in monasteries.

* Always check with your doctor if you have dreams that refer to personal ill health.

Month 11
Creative Spirituality

Spirituality is the ability of the human mind to transcend, to go beyond the limits of time and space. Many systems of belief seek to offer us a vision of existence in which material limitations are transcended by the potential of the soul. This chapter shows you how to open yourself to the transcendent and how to tune into the spiritual dimension of existence.

We see spirituality in language, ethics, humor, creativity, systems of belief, and our desire to understand the mysteries of our world. The disciplines of meditation, prayer, retreat, and pilgrimage demand perseverance and dedication. This month we also learn how to listen to our inner guru.

The eleventh path

A cardinal number, eleven is a team number. Football, hockey, and cricket are all played with eleven people. In Creative Spirituality we learn the importance of supporting others and, in return, receiving support.

According to some numerologists, eleven symbolizes transition. Keep the number in mind when traveling from the physical to the spiritual worlds. As we near the end of our creative year, consider the concept of the eleventh hour. Is there any last-minute business that you need to address?

Questionnaire

✳ What beliefs do you hold about a divine presence in your life?

✳ Are these beliefs ones that you were taught as a child?

✳ Have you felt a sensation of being one with the world?

✳ Do you feel that you are more than your physical entity?

✳ Have you ever experienced a sense of wonder in natural surroundings?

Feedback

• Divine means many things. It relates to God, Allah, or any other deity. It is associated with worship and excellence or supreme worth, and we may recognize divinity by intuition or insight. Whatever your beliefs, religious or otherwise, you may sense the presence of something greater in your life than yourself. In this section we will explore ways of being more open to the divine in daily life.

• Early teaching of religious beliefs may be a blessing or a hindrance, according to your personal experience. It is useful to think about how basic values enhance your life rather than focus on any negative experiences with teachers or religious leaders. Look at core values, which usually include love of others as well as yourself.

• For many, love of nature is at the center of spiritual experience. When we appreciate the natural world we are connected to the divine.

• The transcendent feeling of being at one with the world is a spiritual experience that lets us know that our energy is the same energy that is in a tree, a river, and another person. We are all energy and we are all one.

- A sense of gratitude for life, even in the difficult times, allows us to hope and to honor the power of life. Where we experience grace in this way the spiritual dimension of our being can flourish.

- Whether or not you believe in life after death, you can be more than your physical entity because the love and kindness you give to others lives on even though you are not present physically.

Caring for your soul

There is an inner computer far more sensitive than any machine. The soul knows how to compute its own destiny and, if it is given a chance, how to achieve it.
From *Dancing in the Flames* by MARION WOODMAN and ELINOR DICKSON

The soul is that aspect of ourselves that far goes beyond the surface self to that which lies within. It represents the spiritual side of ourselves, not our physical or material needs, and connects us to the divine, though it need not be attached to any particular religious tradition. We each need to learn to hear the whispers of our soul, which sometimes come in dreams.

Care of the Soul, by Thomas Moore, psychotherapist and former Catholic monk, teaches that spirituality is part of everyday life. The sacred can be found in the ordinary, so each moment of the day can become a moment of spiritual growth and mystical awareness.

Caring for your soul starts with the law adhered to by physicians for over 2,400 years: "First do no harm." By embracing the following approaches you will increase the amount of love you send to, and receive from, others:

- Say only what is kind and helpful to yourself and to others.

- Give only positive messages to yourself and others. Try not to be sarcastic, tart, brusque, dismissive, or aggressive.

- Give your full attention to any person you meet. Whether they are a storekeeper or your best friend, give them your undivided attention and notice how the quality of your listening and empathy is increased.

- Treat yourself with loving-kindness. Nurture the breath of your soul; the energy will continue after your physical self has ended.

Keep these sentences in mind for an hour or a morning, and make some notes in your Creative Year Journal on how they make you feel. What made this activity easier? What made it harder?

Finding the spirit within

Angels fly because they take themselves so lightly.
G. K. CHESTERTON

Intuition awakens us to the spiritual dimension of life and lets us meet our souls. It gives us information that guides us away from danger and toward grace. As we saw earlier, intuition provides insights and awareness on many practical matters, but in this section we will discover the part that intuition plays in our spirituality. All major religions speak of God or the divine as an "indwelling spirit," within each and every one of us.

The spirit within has different names in different religions and cultures. Hindus call it the "inner guru," for Tibetan Buddhists it is the "personal deity," Christian Quakers say "the still, small voice within," and psychologists use the term "higher self." When seeking the spirit within, it is best to set aside some time from your daily routine to go on a "vision quest." You do not necessarily need to clear forty days and forty nights from your diary, but free up as much space as possible for your sacred journey. If you cannot take off on a trip, then set aside an hour to greet your higher self.

* Take some time to relax and turn your attention inward.

* Review your life. Have there been any moments in your life when you have felt an inner guide communicating with you or when you felt a presence walking beside you? Often this happens at times of great stress.

* Invite your inner guide to come to you now. What question do you wish to ask? What reply do you receive?

* You can continue your dialogue. Make a note of your feelings and words in your Creative Year Journal.

A candle to light the darkness

Darkness is necessary for life and essential for growth and protection. In the darkness of the earth seeds germinate, and darkness comes to soothe sun-drenched deserts. However, for many of us darkness—the black of an unlit room or the metaphorical dark night of the soul—is frightening.

Candles have been used for thousands of years and come in all shapes and sizes. Some are even impregnated with aromatic oils. They are used in religious festivals, rituals, and celebrations.

The following activity is to help you embrace the power of light and illuminate your darkness.

* Choose a time of darkness when all around is quiet.

* Place a lighted candle in a safe, comfortable area. Turn off any other lighting and sit in front of the candle.

* As you watch the flame, absorb its brilliance. Note how such a small flame can spread its light and illuminate the space.

* Think about a dark part in your life and imagine light being cast on that area.

* Sit quietly and remember that times of darkness are often times of great personal and spiritual growth.

* Bring your thoughts back to the present moment and make an affirmation: "My world is brightened by healing light."

Mandala making

Mandalas, sacred circles, have been used for centuries as an aid to contemplation and concentration. The diagrams represent the sacred map of the cosmos and are spiritual and psychological "maps" in meditation. When looking at a mandala, choose one of the doors at the outer edges and let your eye travel toward the center, which symbolizes the completed path, the unified state of being where your physical, emotional, and spiritual self is at one.

Mandalas are works of devotion rather than ambition and are painted on scrolls known as tankas. They are collective acts not credited to named artists because the makers are not concerned with ego or pride. Tibetan sand mandalas take days to complete and are then blown away. This symbolizes the impermanence of all things.

In Marin General Hospital in California, mandala drawing is part of the Humanities Healing Project offered to both patients and the wider community. In the following activity, we will explore the potential of healing through making a mandala.

* Make a photocopy of a mandala that you like.
* Look at the mandala in minute detail. Notice the entrances and follow the intricate paths to its heart.
* Draw and color your own mandala made to your own design.

Practical spirituality

To bow to the fact of our life's sorrows and betrayals is to accept them; and from this deep gesture we discover that all life is workable. As we learn to bow, we discover that the heart holds more freedom and compassion than we could imagine.

From *After the Ecstasy, the Laundry* by JACK KORNFIELD

American author and meditation teacher Jack Kornfield, the writer of *The Path with a Heart* and *After the Ecstasy, the Laundry*, tells a wonderful story about how he became a Buddhist monk in a forest monastery in Thailand. He describes bowing to all monks who were ordained before him, and, as he was the most recently ordained, that meant everyone. He learned to find something in each person to value and venerate, from the wrinkles of a retired rice farmer to the playful energy of young monks who were only there to please their parents. What he learned from this is that spirituality is not somewhere romantic and remote, but in the everyday places and actions that we are living, here and now.

Our spirituality is enhanced as we greet every experience with respect and tolerance. Washing the dishes, peeling the potatoes, or emptying the garbage are all sacred acts; celebrate the work that others have put into making the objects that decorate our households, harvesting the crops we eat, and removing the waste from our neighborhoods. Kornfield describes this as bowing to what is rather than to an ideal.

Passion and compassion

Spiritual care is promoted through being there for others, being compassionate, and holding on to hope when all hope seems to have gone. In compassion we feel for others, we empathize, and we want to alleviate their suffering. The word "compassion" comes from a compound of two Latin words *com* (with) and *pati* (to suffer) meaning "to suffer with." The first part of the word is compass, the instrument we use to find our direction. Often in compassion we find spiritual direction because the path of compassion connects us to all people and creatures that inhabit our world.

✳ For five days write down the most important thing that happened each day. Include any feelings of passion and compassion.

✳ On the sixth day look through your record. Often the things that are most important are not the "big" things but the simple ones. The everyday events that shape our lives, the fresh smell of the earth after rain, the rainbow slick on a puddle, the smile of a child in a shop as she clutches a balloon.

✳ What does your record tell you about your passion and compassion? What fires you and touches your heart?

✳ On the seventh day celebrate the fact that you know more about your innermost feelings and consider how you can make more room for the important things in your life.

The power of intentionality

My true religion is kindness.   THE FOURTEENTH DALAI LAMA OF TIBET

Prayer is an act of faith. It may be linked to religious practice, but it doesn't have to be. In praying, there is the sense of giving yourself over to a greater power, an acceptance that there is more than ourselves in this world, even though we do not understand and cannot explain what else there could be. Through prayer we open ourselves up to tuning into other people and other places.

In his book *Healing Words: The Power of Prayer and the Practice of Medicine*, Dr. Larry Dossey reveals evidence to show how prayers said for a sick person help in the healing process. These prayers can be said in locations far from the patient and by those who do not have religious affiliations. In order to make your prayers beneficial, you need to hold your intention in your heart and mind and concentrate on a positive outcome. What you think matters and, in a way, each thought is a prayer.

In Tibet people write their prayers on flags made of triangles of cloth. The flags are then attached to a rope or string and placed outside homes and temples. Every time the wind blows the prayers are sent into the world. Prayer wheels are also used. A prayer is written on a scroll and put inside the wheel. Every time the wheel is turned, intentions are dispersed.

* Choose a quiet, comfortable place and breathe deeply. Once you feel calm and relaxed turn your attention inward.

* Think about a situation you would like to change. This may be about your own or someone else's health, a relationship, or a work issue.

* Frame an intention or prayer—"Please let me find the strength to get through this loss" or "May my father's health improve once his operation is complete"— whatever is important to you. Say the words to yourself or out loud.

* Notice the feelings that arise as you say the words. Make a note in your Creative Year Journal of your prayer and your feelings.

Touching the divine

If we take eternity to mean not infinite temporal duration but timelessness, then eternal life belongs to those who live in the present. WITTGENSTEIN

The American poet Ralph Waldo Emerson expressed the idea of an oversoul, a universal spirit that is in everything. It was the duty of everyone to follow the path of transcendentalism and become part of this overarching spirituality. In doing this, Emerson argued, it was important to be self-directed and self-reliant; people should follow the intuition they received from the Universal Spirit and mix with others in order to gain a wide experience of the world.

Open a window through which divinity can touch your life, whoever or whatever you believe it to be. This moment is all we have, and it is precious. We still look to the future, we have our hopes and dreams, but cherishing the moment is essential. The following exercise lets you celebrate the moment and accept its transience.

✳ Visit a snowy plain, a sandy beach, a mud flat, or a wet street.

✳ On the surface you have chosen, walk out the name of someone you love.

✳ Let each footfall connect you to the person you have chosen.

✳ On completion, watch how the surface absorbs your creation.

✳ See how the earth contains your heart.

Contemplative silence

Irish writer John O'Donohue wrote a powerful book called *Anam Cara*, which is Gaelic for "soul friend." He says that there is a massive spiritual hunger since "old shelters for the psyche, like religion, have collapsed." We still need the spiritual dimension that we find in many places, including contemplative silence.

If the mind is free, the creative side can flow. In this activity you are going to clear a space in your routine so that, in the silence of the mind, deeper awareness of the transcendent may arise.

* Choose a quiet space where you will be undisturbed for at least fifteen minutes.

* Take a few deep breaths, then let your breathing quietly ease into a relaxed rhythm.

* Choose a spiritually significant word or phrase and quietly turn your attention to it. This could be "light," "peace," "joy," "heaven," or "the word of God."

* Think about the word or phrase; be aware of any feelings or connections it brings up. If you find your mind wandering off at a tangent, gently bring your attention back and repeat your word and phrase again.

* After ten minutes, write down any thoughts and feelings that arose. Notice how, when you give yourself contemplative silence, your mind can bring so much to your attention.

Meditation

Meditation is the practice of stilling the mind and may involve sitting still or walking and watching your breath with the aim of developing concentration and avoiding distractions. There are many forms of meditation and contemplation, and each may lead to profound spiritual experiences and bliss. "Bliss," as Roger Walsh says in his book *Essential Spirituality*, "is the taste of our spiritual nature." This may come through meditation, painting, walking in nature, helping others who are sick, or sitting at rest after a day of fulfilling work. Bliss can happen at any point if we are open to it.

Pilgrimage

Caring for your soul may involve going on a pilgrimage. Sacred sites are found across the globe: Uluru in Australia, Santiago de Compostela in Spain, Mount Tai in China, and Varanasi in India are just a handful of the thousands of places of pilgrimage.

Our earliest ancestors made maps of the world in which they lived, as well as other maps of the journeys their spirits took. Examples of soul maps can be found in the Paleolithic cave art of Europe and in the depths of caverns in Africa. In Australia, the United States and Siberia, shamans, or medicine men and women, plotted the journeys to divinity. Their maps show a connection to people and places far away, perhaps only dreamed of, and they illustrate the lasting importance of creative mark-making to the human journey.

✷ Over the next few weeks, find out about pilgrimage sites. Gather some information about their significance—find maps of the area and any details that appeal to you.

✷ Choose one site. In your Creative Year Journal write down the reasons you would like to visit that particular place and what you would hope to attain while you were there.

✷ Make a map of your journey from your home to your chosen site.

Giving and receiving

Often we find it hard to intentionally offer something to ourselves. The following activity involves you giving or offering to others and to yourself. To give is also to receive. When we give to others part of ourselves is uplifted; when we offer love part of our own mind is first filled with love as we imagine giving it.

* Find yourself a quiet space where you can be alone for fifteen minutes. Breathe deeply and be aware of a calm feeling flooding your body.

* When you are ready think about what you want to offer to others you care about. Among these gifts might be: "I offer love to my friends"; "I offer contentment to my family"; "I offer peace to my neighbors"; or "I offer hope to my friend."

* Now make the same offers to yourself.

* You can extend this activity to your community, your country, and to the world.

Month 12

Creative Completion

You have arrived at the final path in your year of creativity. Now is the time to reflect, to consider how these paths have taken you to places of invention and creativity, to sites of special significance in your life's journey. It is now time to weave together the creative strands that make up your personal tapestry of mind, body, and spirit so you can complete the greater picture.

Completion takes us to the point in the cycle of life where we begin again, for completion is part of a process and not an end in itself. In *The Search for the Panchen Lama*, Isabel Hilton tells how she was leaving a park in Beijing when she saw an old man writing Chinese characters in a packed dirt path. He dipped a long-handled brush in water and wrote the lines of a Tang poem in exquisite calligraphy. As he got to the end of the poem, as he reached completion, the first words he'd written had been absorbed and disappeared. He did not need to leave permanent traces for others to see. The creative process was enough in itself.

Isabel, a Chinese scholar, accepted his offer of the brush and added a line from a classic Daoist poem: "The way that can be known is not the constant way." Transience and renewal are part of our completion.

The twelfth path

Twelve is a number associated with counselors, prophets, and disciples. The Twelvers are a sect of a Shiite branch of Muslims. They recognize twelve imams or religious leaders who have descended from Ali, the Prophet Mohammed's cousin and son-in-law. In Christianity, Jesus chose twelve apostles to teach his gospel. There were twelve founders of the tribes of Israel. The people of ancient Greece worshiped twelve principal deities: Zeus, Hera, Aphrodite, Ares, Hephaestus, Artemis, Hestia, Poseidon, Apollo, Demeter, Athena, and Hermes. This month look at increasing the number of people who can teach your creative spirit. Think also if there is anyone else in your life who could benefit from the lessons you have learned over the last year.

Twelfth Night is traditionally a time of great merrymaking. Make sure that you celebrate your newfound creativity at this stage of your journey.

Questionnaire

* What have you enjoyed about your creative experiences in A Year of Creativity?

* What have you learned about your ability to begin and complete activities?

* Have you noticed anything that holds you back, such as not making time or fear that you might not be good enough?

✳ What has been the highlight of your creative year?

✳ What do you want to say to the creative spirit that is you?

Feedback

• As we complete our creative year it is time to look back. We think about all that has happened, what we have completed, and what we wish to begin. In the process of many activities you have discovered much about yourself.

• Your answers to this questionnaire reflect your journey to this point, its lows and highs, each of which provide an opportunity for creative growth. We are learning and gathering wisdom about ourselves and the world in which we live.

• By now you will know more about the creative spirit that is you, since you have had many opportunities to let it play away from the glare of censorship and external judgment. Now is the time to acclaim that side of yourself and here are some extra affirmations to help to add to what you said to your creative spirit:

✳ I welcome the joy my creative side brings to my life.

✳ I trust the creative process that fills my day.

✳ I open my heart to the creative spirit that dwells within.

✳ Traveling with my creative spirit brings meaning to my life.

The heart's path

In a full heart there is room for everything while in an empty heart there is room for nothing. ANTONIO PORCHIA

As we travel the path of life there are peak experiences that gladden our hearts and troughs that make our hearts sink. You will have already identified many of these as you completed earlier activities. From both the slough of despond and the magnificence of heartfelt love you can learn more about your heart's path.

In your Creative Year Journal write down answers to the following questions:

✳ What have you learned from your peak experiences?
✳ What have you learned from your low points?
✳ What patterns can you see?

The heart's path is a path of love. This love encompasses family, friends, teachers, lovers, partners, children, and whatever is important to you. If love has been rejected it does not mean you must reject yourself, merely that the person to whom it was offered had not the wisdom to accept it.

Consider your heart's journey. What was it closed to that it is open to now? Travel the path that lets your heart beat freely, where you can be open about your feelings and share with others. Only then can the true creative self emerge. Those who lack the courage to let their heart love are oppressed by feelings of anger, bitterness, and cruelty, which is a loss for everyone. The path of the heart is the path of compassion.

Celebration

He who can believe himself, will be well.   OVID

The creative act of celebration brings joy and laughter and causes life-enhancing endorphins to flood our bodies, which in turn build up our immune system. You will have discovered many aspects of your life that are worthy of celebration from your Creative Year Journal.

Look through your journal once more and recall any points where joy roars and laughter resonates.

There is a story of a man who had lived a full and happy life. He knew death was approaching and he told his family, "I know it won't be long now but I want to go out laughing, so I want you to think about the times we laughed. In the time left I want to hear your stories and I'll tell you some too." That's what they did and he died with a smile on his lips.

What stories about your life make you smile? What stories would you like others to tell you?

Reconciliation

To understand is to forgive.   FRENCH PROVERB

In your Creative Year Journal you may have recorded times in the past with people who have caused you pain. You may have lashed out in anger, severed friendships, or become estranged from family members. Your feelings may have been justifiable, but when we harbor feelings of anger they gnaw away at us and create more distress for ourselves.

If you look back in order to understand rather than to blame or plan revenge, you can begin the process of freeing your energy for more important aspects of your life. People do the best they can with the knowledge and experience they have at the time. Revisit the events of one of those painful points and try to understand what motivated the other person and yourself at that time. Fear, anxiety, pride, and lack of understanding are common participants when people fall out. This does not mean you accept what happened or that it makes it right, it means that you seek to understand what happened and then let go. If you don't let go of those ties that bind you to the painful past they become bonds that trap you. Choose to let go in a spirit of reconciliation.

The importance of the worst time

What is broken does not always mend in the same way, but becomes mossed over in a different shape.

From *Ann of Bedlam Her Book* by CLARE CROSSMAN

In your Creative Year Journal you may have recorded failures. These may represent relationships that ended unhappily, missed opportunities, or simply the inability to produce a drawing you wanted to make. Take heart—failure is a vital part of the creative process.

The freedom to fail is underrated. We learn so much about ourselves and the world when things turn out other than how we planned. This precious right of failure allows us to try, to push the envelope. Failure can teach us to become more detached, to let go of arrogant expectations. Success is not always in our best interests. Failure can also purify our motives. Do we really need whatever it was that seemed so important to us? Will the world fall apart if we are unsuccessful?

Catastrophes, an "out of the blue" accident, a life-threatening illness, the loss of a loved partner, force us to stop and take stock. They cause us to think about the life we are leading and hasten the process that Jung termed "individuation," that is learning what we want to do with our lives to become the person we were meant to be.

Grace and grit

In a Native American healing ceremony, the healer asks a series of questions: "When in your life did you stop singing?" "When in your life did you stop dancing?" "When in your life did you lose enchantment with story?" "When in your life did you start to feel uncomfortable with your sacred silence?"

These are questions we all need to ask ourselves, whether we are sick or not. We need to sing and dance, to step lightly as we tread our giving earth. We need our myths and stories as we discovered in the section on Creative Writing. We need the power of time apart to listen, in the silence, to the whispers of our soul.

Sometimes we need the grit of gutsy determination to keep going. British mountaineer Joe Simpson had a horrific experience when climbing in the Himalayas. Alone on the mountain, left for dead, he dragged himself, inch by inch, toward the base camp. Death appeared to be imminent, yet he forced himself to carry on despite unbearable pain. When asked in an interview what made him keep going he replied, "I kept crawling, I just kept crawling, because I didn't want to do it alone. I wanted someone to hold me." With grit comes grace, which is always permeated with love.

Weaving the strands of your life

Throughout the exercises on writing, abundance, and visualization, you will have discovered strands of your history. Friendships, jobs, travel, and domestic life have all braided together to make the person you are now.

The following activity, which is based on the idea of "bringing in," weaves together those strands of your history.

* Look back through your Creative Year Journal. Take extracts that fall into the following five categories:

  • What I like about myself.
  • Nuggets of beauty from difficult times.
  • Places and people who have made a difference to my life.
  • Joyous words and affirmations.
  • Anything else that feels enriching.

* Set your extracts out on paper, using different colors and different lines, until you make a tapestry to complete the picture so far.

* Remember that the future will bring you threads of gold and silver to add to your weaving as your life becomes richer and more deeply layered. All strands, light or dark, rough or smooth, are part of the person you are.

Endings as beginnings

Until you know about death how can you know about life?

CONFUCIUS

For the Ancient Egyptians, Ba was the human soul, depicted as a bird or a bird with a human body. Ba symbolized the idea that after death the soul could fly off, like a bird, and join the ancestors. Small passageways connected tombs to the outside world so that souls could come and go in the life after death. So the death of the human body was the beginning of a new journey for the soul.

Life, so-called, is a short episode between two great mysteries, which yet are one. CARL JUNG

Every end, whether it is a completed job, a cooked meal, or a written letter, is also a beginning. A finished task frees time for rest or another activity, a meal prepared signals a time to begin eating, and a posted letter is received and so a process of communication begins afresh. Completion is a part of a cyclical process, which is eternal, and we all share in that unending process.

The wisdom of years

Memories live on in our bodies as well as the material objects that surround us. As we age, though we usually feel that we are still in our twenties, the mirror reveals a parent. "I looked in the mirror and I saw my mother," is the shocked cry many women make. Thomas Hardy's poem "Heredity" (1917) captures this and takes it on to the eternal connection we have to our families.

> *I am the family face;*
> *Flesh perishes, I live on,*
> *Projecting trait and trace*
> *Through time to times anon,*
> *And leaping from place to place*
> *Over oblivion.*

Whatever your age now, embrace the wisdom that has become part of you. You can be wiser at twenty than a seventy-year-old who is closed off from new experiences. In your wisdom, consider what words you would give to another to help them on their life path.

Giving yourself permission to shine

Imagine yourself on a glorious mountain peak. A bright sun shines on you and illuminates you against a clear blue sky. Shout out what you feel pleased to have achieved so far:

* I kept my heart open when everyone told me I was a fool.

* I loved the earth and tended my garden.

* I make a difference in other people's lives.

Recognizing your strengths is sometimes less acceptable than announcing your weaknesses, but remember, the more we talk about "failings" the more we reinforce negative images of ourselves. Try to refocus your attention on your positive potential. Bring your creative abilities to the service of yourself and others. When you shine in the world you bring brightness to everyone's life.

And in the end, Love is all there is.
Love is All.
At the beginning. In the End
Love is all that matters,
And what matters, is love.   BRENDA MALLON

Picture Credits

All antique embroidered textile images appear courtesy of Linda Wrigglesworth Ltd., London, copyright © Linda Wrigglesworth, Ltd.

p. 2, 109, 135, 142 Early 19th century Imperial Yellow Empress' chaofu. **p. 10** 19th century Manchu woman's embroidered winter robe depicting "the three friends" and shou symbols. **p. 12, 35** Embroidered Souchao hanging depicting birds and flowers in the islands of Penglai. **p. 25, 65, 81, 168, 251** 18th century Kesi weave scroll depicting the eight immortals, the three stars of happiness, and the goddess of the West, Xi Wangmu arriving on a phoenix. **p. 36, 173** 19th century detail of a Europeon paddle steamer. **p. 47, 189** Detail of embroidery depicting a dignitary and his wife receiving gifts. **p. 58** 18th century flag for a ship's mast depicting a flying tiger, the emblem of Emperor Kangxi's navel regiment. **p. 61, 100, 222** Detail of a woman's sur-coat embroidered with a circular crane surrounded by bats holding peaches, symbols of longevity. **p. 75, 97, 159, 238** 19th century Han woman's silk robe. **p. 82** 19th century Manchu woman's silk embroidered late summer robe. **p. 84** Detail on red silk of two scholars visiting the home of another scholar. **p. 87** Back of a Taoist priest's robe embroidered with four of the eight trigams, a mandala of the Universe, sun and moon constellations, and the pagoda from the mountains of Penglai. **p. 90** 18th century roundel from a scholar's robe. **p. 93** 19th century badge of office for a military officer, depicting leopards. **p. 103, 160** Military badge of a 2nd rank officer depicting a lion. **p. 106** Pair of 19th century embroidered chair covers. **p. 113, 183** Detail of a wall hanging embroidered in Pekin knot depicting the one hundred scholar's objects. **p. 119, 204** Detail from and 18th century wall hanging of three Mandarins displaying their badges of office on official duty. **p. 120, 201** 19th century Han Chinese woman's silk jacket embroidered with roundels. **p. 124** Detail from 18th century wall hanging depicting an egret and a rock. **p. 126** 17th century Sino-Tibetan embroidery of a dakini flying through the heavens emanating a rainbow. **p. 140** 18th century Chinese European style tapestry depicting views across a landscape. **p. 150** Late 19th century Manchu woman's gauze silk robe embroidered with lotus and lily pads. **p. 153** Late 19th century Manchu court woman's robe embroidered with wisteria and butterflies. **p. 154** Informal Mandarin winter robe of cut velvet, woven with roundels of elephants. **p. 156** Detail of a robe made for the Empress Cixi, embroidered with peonies and symbols of good luck and longevity. **p. 164** Manchu woman's robe woven with butterflies to symbolize happiness. **p. 179** 18th century Sino-Tibetan altar frontal embroidered with Buddhist symbols. **p. 184** Celebration hanging from the great hall of a Mandarin house. **p. 206** Pair of 19th century badges of office worn by a first rank Mandarin. **p. 245** 19th century altar hanging embroidered with a scene of a group of scholars visiting an old friend.

Resources

Affiliation of Crystal Healing Organizations
46 Lower Green Road
Esher
Surrey KT10 8HD
UK

American Holistic Medical Association
Suite 201
4101 Lake Boone Tail
Raleigh NC 27607
USA

Association for the Study of Dreams
P.O. Box 1592
Merced
CA 95341-1592
USA
www.ASDreams.org

The Buzan Centres USA Inc.
PO Box 4
Palm Beach
FL 33480.
USA

Centre for Transpersonal Psychology
7–11 Kensington High Street
London W8 5NP
UK
Courses in transpersonal psychology,
visualization, and dreams.

Colour Therapy Association
P.O. Box 16576
London SW20 8ZW
UK

Judith Cornell, Ph.D.
Manifesting Inner Light
P.O. Box 517
Sausalito
CA 94966-0517
USA
e-mail: ommandala@aol.com

Creative Therapies for Life
Brenda Mallon
e-mail: lapwing@gn.apc.org
www.brendamallon.com

Schumacher College
The Old Postern
Dartington, Totnes
Devon TQ9 6EA
UK
e-mail: schumcoll@gn.apc.org
www.gn.apc.org/schumachercollege/
Courses in spirituality, creativity, ecology, and
sustainability.

Pauline Wills
The Oracle School of Colour
9 Wyndale Avenue, Kingsbury
London NW9 9PT
UK

Text Credits

Note: Every care has been taken to contact copyright owners. The editor would be pleased to hear from any copyright holders not acknowledged below, and will make corrections in any future edition.

p. 198 Excerpt from *The Therapeutic Potential of Creative Writing: Writing Myself* by Gillie Bolton. London: Jessica Kingsley, 1999. **p. 91** Excerpt from *The Waste Land* by T. S. Eliot. New York: Boni and Liveright, 1922. **p. 136** Excerpt from *Letters from a Young Poet* by Rainer Maria Rilke. Copyright © 2000. Used with permission from New World Library, Novato, CA 94949, www.newworldlibrary.com.

Acknowledgments

To Django Mallon, the newest creation.

I would like to thank all those people, teachers, friends, clients, and workshop participants who have shown me how creativity can change our world. Their inspiration, laughter, insights, and persistence made this book possible.

Thanks to Slaney and Leanne for wonderful editorial support. And finally, unending gratitude as ever to the sustaining love of Styx, Karl, Crystal, and Danny.